AF593387

DISCIPLE
IN BLUE
SUEDE
SHOES

DISCIPLE IN BLUE SUEDE SHOES

CARL PERKINS

with
RON RENDLEMAN

ZONDERVAN PUBLISHING HOUSE OF THE ZONDERVAN CORPORATION GRAND RAPIDS, MICHIGAN 49506

DISCIPLE IN BLUE SUEDE SHOES

Grand Rapids, Michigan

Library of Congress Cataloging in Publication Data

Perkins, Carl.
Disciple in blue suede shoes.

1. Perkins, Carl. 2. Country musicians—United States—Biography. 3. Christian biography —United States. I. Title.
ML420.P453A3 784'.092'4 [B] 78-57518
ISBN 0-310-36730-1

Printed in the United States of America

I dedicate this book to its true author, Jesus Christ. I did not in reality write it. Only after searching prayer could I find the words to express what He wanted me to. I had only eight years of formal education, and my spelling and punctuation are not what they should be. God knew I needed help, and He supplied it. My family encouraged me to accomplish God's will. They prayed for me and helped me in every way possible. My sons typed and my daughter helped me put my thoughts into words. Then God sent Ron Rendleman to help us organize and rework the material into a book.

I thank God for allowing me to tell my story and to Him I give the glory.

Contents

You may know him as the composer of the fifties hit, *Blue Suede Shoes,* or later, *Daddy Sang Bass,* or the man who, with soul on fire, sang and danced on table tops of southern honky-tonks. You may know him as the man who performed in Johnny Cash's road show for ten years or as the man who turned his life over to Christ on Easter Sunday, 1966.

I know him as Daddy, the man who gave me living proof that Jesus Christ is alive. His life was not uncluttered by snarls and tangles, and you might well be skeptical of how a man so harassed by Satan, so seemingly abandoned by God, could emerge with any faith at all.

But, come, walk along with us a spell and listen to Carl Perkins tell us himself why he's traveling a brand-new road these days. Afterward, as you continue your own life's journey, perhaps you, too, will want to change direction a little.

DEBRA PERKINS SWIFT

Carl Perkins is a Christian. He is also an entertainer and one of the greatest. His calling is that he be in the world, yet unworldly. He performs in concert halls, city auditoriums, and at times in places Christian brothers might refer to as dens of iniquity. Yet it is in these places that Carl's calling is the toughest and probably most effective, for he remains a Christian, never compromising his testimony wherever he is. Carl's calling isn't easy, but then the Lord never said it was going to be.

I have been "down the road" with Carl Perkins. I know him as a Christian, as a friend, and as a brother. I thought I knew everything about him; then I read this book. It inspired me and it touched me as he laid bare that beautiful country soul.

If you ever saw him perform, he moved you to tap your toes. This "Disciple in Blue Suede Shoes" will move you to more spiritual heights.

JOHNNY CASH

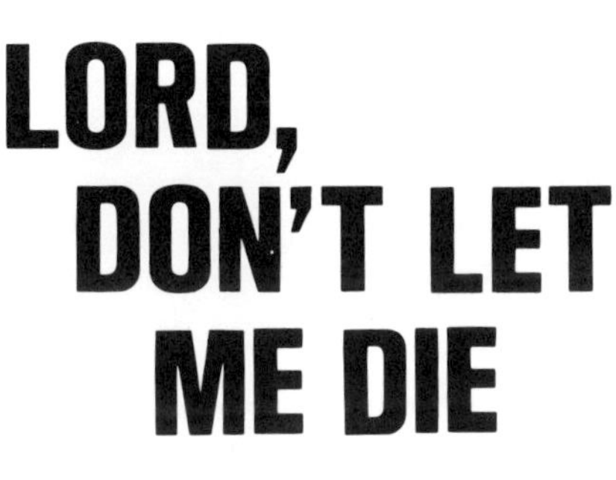

LORD, DON'T LET ME DIE

I was sitting alone in my dressing room at the Shrine Auditorium in San Diego, drunk and crying. Outside 12,000 fans were rhythmically clapping for the overdue show to begin. But I was too drunk to go on. I wanted to die. I had promised myself, my family, and God that this was one thing that would never happen—but it had. I had been touring with Johnny Cash.

My job was to warm up the audience with three or four songs, assisted by Marshall Grant on bass, Luther Perkins on guitar, and W. S. Holland on drums, and then Johnny would make his entrance. For years I had been able to perform under the influence—it took away stage jitters, sort of put spice into my act—but this time I had gone too far. I couldn't even stand up.

"Carl?" Johnny Cash stuck his head in the room. "How come you're not out there? The crowd's gettin' fidgety." I looked up at my friend. "I cain't, John. I drunk too much."

He pulled up a chair, smiling. "Ah, champ, you can do it. All you got to do is sing three songs. You don't have to say nothin'. Just walk out there and *do* it—I know you can, 'cause you're the King."

I looked long and hard at my friend. He believed in me. He really believed I could pull it off. I knew I could easily make a fool of myself by going out there, maybe even ruin my career. But if I didn't, John wouldn't be giving the customers all they had paid to see. Besides, through the years that we'd been friends, never once had either one let the other down. I had to do it. I took a deep breath to clear my head. I stood up but started to fall backward till a chair held me. Somehow I got my guitar out of the case and the strap around my shoulder. I tuned it a little and nodded to John, and he led the way out to the stage.

I walked up to the microphone, but I could see nothing but a blinding haze of colored lights. I rushed through *Blue Suede Shoes* and two others, hoping no one would suspect, but you don't hide a staggering step and slurred words. Even though it was a bad performance, no one booed, and when I had finished I shoved my way past the crowd standing in the wings and out the back door of the auditorium. I was so ashamed! I was crying as I found my way to John's motor home parked in the back lot and managed to climb in and fall across the bed. I vaguely remember the bus returning to our motel, laying on my own bed, seeing a blinking liquor sign, and staggering out to buy a pint.

The next morning I awoke in the back of Johnny's bus, not having any idea how I got there. Dimly I could make out the sounds of laughter outside somewhere. June Carter and John were up front. June must have heard me moaning.

"How you feeling, Carl?" she asked, leaning over me.

"Not so good. I feel like dying." And I meant it.

"Carl, John wanted to die, too. But look at him now. Why don't you do what he did. Call on God. He'll help you."

"I don't deserve to live," I cried. "I ought to die. God cain't love me any more."

"Oh, yes He does," she said. "You talk to Him. John and I'll let you be. When you feel up to it, come join us and the others. We're fixin' to have a picnic. John drove us to a nice spot by the ocean."

I lay there alone for a long time, slipping in and out of consciousness. Once I tried to get up but couldn't—a forceful hand seemed to shove me down. I was sick to my stomach, my head was spinning, and, in my stupor, I was sure fuzzy, big-eyed bugs were crawling all over me. I'd never experienced such horror before—I was scared! Was I dying? I started praying aloud. "Lord, I don't have the right to ask You to let me live, but, Lord, if I'm dying, let me live long enough to get home to see Val and my little kids. Let them see me sober, but don't let me die here, like this."

After awhile I began to feel a little better. I looked around and spotted my brown tote bag on the floor. I knew what was in that tote bag. I reached over for it and found my nearly full pint of whiskey from the night before. I was lifting the bottle to my lips when a very real, but inaudible voice interrupted me. *Carl, you asked Me to let you make it home, but if you take one drink you'll never see your family again.* I knew who was speaking. It was the One I had ignored most of my life. I couldn't risk ignoring Him any longer. I put the cap back on the bottle, struggled to my feet, and groped my way through the bus. Just when I got to the front, John climbed in.

"Are you still drinking, Carl?" he asked, looking at the bottle I was starting to put in my hip pocket.

"No, John," I answered. "I've decided that if I can walk off this bus, I'm going to throw this bottle away."

"Come on, I'll help you," he said.

"No, I'm going to do it myself," I said. "If you can do it, so can I. He's my God, too."

Somehow, I made it outside. I was standing on a blazing white beach. Lying vast and magnificent before me was the Pacific Ocean. Members of the group were swimming, playing, having a great time. I went off by myself to a secluded place down near the water, looked out across that ocean, a breath-taking testimony to God's handiwork, and thought about the commitment I had made a year earlier on Easter Sunday. My wife, Val, and I and the kids were in our church, the Bemis Methodist Church in Jackson, Tennessee. The preacher gave an invitation for us to give our lives to God. Val, my son Stan, and my daughter Debbie stood up and waited for me to let them by. I let them out and watched them walk that aisle, and then God spoke to me. *Carl, you come, too. I want you to confess before everyone in this church that you believe in Me. You know you do.*

For years I had been staggering around in life, a nominal Christian, gaining a step and falling back two, a slave to the bottle, half a husband, half a father, and I knew it was because I was serving the wrong lord. I started to break out in perspiration. My heart was pounding. I did believe in Jesus Christ, but the lord I had been serving was blocking the way out of that pew. But I would not be stopped—not this time. I got out into the aisle and almost ran to join my family who were down in front on their knees.

And now as I stood on the warm California sand, God reminded me of that vow. I reached into my back pocket and pulled out the bottle and studied it. After a moment I got on my knees.

"Lord, I let You down. I told You I'd never drink again. I'm gonna' have to have You in order not to. I know I can't do this all by myself. Help me, Lord." As I stood up and threw that devil's brew far out into the ocean, I knew I had broken his power in my life and great joy swept over me.

I sat down on the warm sand and watched sea gulls diving into the surf. A cool ocean breeze caressed my cheek, the sun warmed my back, and I felt like I was in heaven. I can't describe the strength that seemed to be lifting me high—as high as the gulls circling overhead.

I lay on my back in the sand and let the sun bore into my face and chest. And then the first doubts came. Doubts that just as all the other times, I would fail this time, too. Many a night during the years I was with John, he and I would sit in back of his motor home after a show—him with his pills and beer, me with my fifth of bourbon. We'd talk about our lives, our dreams, our failings, and always we'd end up misty-eyed talking about God. Neither of us wanted to lean on crippling habits, but we couldn't seem to face daily life without them. When I first started drinking as a teen, I never dreamed I'd become addicted—no one does, I guess—but it got so bad that I'd put away a fifth a day, couldn't get out of bed without a slug. This went on for over ten years. And every month I'd try to quit.

Then, in October, 1967, we began a tour in Tulsa. When I met John there, I noticed something different.

"Carl," he said to me, "I haven't had a pill in two weeks. June had this fellow Dr. Nat Winston come out to see me. He really helped."

"John, that's great. You stick to your guns. You can lick it," I answered, smiling. But I wasn't so sure he would succeed after so many failures. He was hooked on amphetamines, sometimes as many as twenty-five a day. I have to admit I had mixed emotions. Part of me wanted him to win because I loved him; part of me wanted him to lose because if he did, then I could be consoled that my habit was unbeatable, too. Day after day I watched him, but he kept winning, and now as I lay on the beach I wanted to win, too, more than anything. Perhaps with God on my side and the willingness to admit that without Him I could do nothing, I would succeed.

I began to think about my life—about Val and the kids and all the times I'd let them down, the times my little old boys had to wear worn-out tennis shoes showing their toes, all the broken promises, the money blown on partying—and I knew that if I was going to succeed this time I would have to take each day as it came. No big promises. No big dreams. And I would have to understand myself better. I wasn't sure I really knew how the bottle had become my god. My mind drifted back over my life, searching, examining, remembering how an old friend had planted a seed that enabled me to write a top hit, *Blue Suede Shoes*. And how, even though I had climbed into the national spotlight, so much of me was sinking.

REACHING THE STARS

I started playing in honky-tonks as a teen with my brothers Jay and Clayton. We dreamed of being on the "Grand Ole Opry" someday, but though our sound had a beat that was unique to country music, we had not convinced anyone important that we had it. After awhile a friend, W. S. Holland, started coming to the clubs to hear us and would stand beside Clayton and beat rhythm on the side of Clayton's bass. I encouraged W. S. to learn drums, and he did by listening to records. When he finally joined us, our sound had the added impact of percussion. We began making tapes and sending them to every record company we could locate. Usually they were returned unopened.

One day I was listening to a disc jockey, Bob Neal, from Memphis, play *Blue Moon of Kentucky* sung by Elvis Presley. Elvis was brand-new on the country scene, and I was astonished to hear his new twist to the old Bill Monroe tune. I turned the radio up and shouted to Val, "That sounds just like us playing! I'm gonna find out who put that record out." At last someone was recording country music with a beat.

The disc had been released by Sun Records in Memphis, so in early March, Jay, Clayton, W. S., and I drove there. We spent much of the day heading down one-way streets the wrong way. At last we found ourselves in the parking lot in front of a small recording studio on Union Avenue.

While the boys waited in the car, I walked into the office and asked the secretary, Marion Kisler, "Are you taking auditions?"

"No, I'm sorry, we aren't," she replied.

"Well, my name is Carl Perkins, and I have this band I would like you to hear."

"I'm sorry, Mr. Perkins, but Mr. Phillips is not interested in recording new people. We have all we can handle with this new fellow, Elvis. His records are the hottest thing on the market."

As I thanked her and left, I began to think hard. There had to be a way to get them to hear us, and I had to find it. Suddenly a new Cadillac came roaring into the parking lot. I looked at my brothers and W. S. and smiled. We weren't finished yet. I knew the fellow in the flashy car must be important.

I stopped him just as he was entering the studio. I had never seen a better dressed man—even tie and socks were the exact color of the Cadillac.

"Sir, you're Mr. Phillips, aren't you?" I asked.

"Yes. What can I do for you?"

"Well, Mr. Phillips, my name is Carl Perkins, and I sure would appreciate it if you could listen to our band."

He hesitated a moment, looked at his watch then looked me over good. Suddenly there were no hurting yesterdays, or even idle dreams for tomorrow—Mr. Phillips held it all. "I guess I could listen to a couple of numbers."

We rushed inside and set up our instruments. Jay seemed calmer than the rest of us.

"Jay, sing Mr. Phillips the song you wrote," I said, trying to avoid the responsibility of selling our style.

Jay always sang the slow songs in the clubs and I sang the faster ones. His voice was deep, and he sounded very much like Ernest Tubb. Mr. Phillips picked it up immediately.

"Sorry, boys, there already is an Ernest Tubb. I can't use you." He started back to his office, and I motioned for the boys to remain where they were.

"Mr. Phillips, would you listen to one more song?" I asked.

"Well, go ahead, one more," he answered, hesitantly.

"Hit it, boys!" I shouted. *"Let me take you to the movie, Magg, where I can hold your hand. . . ."*

I sang with all my heart in a new key, reaching for the stars, higher than I'd ever reached before, and a smile spread over Mr. Phillips face.

"I like that fine. Sing it again. This time, Carl, try to keep still. They can't see you jumping on a record."

But I couldn't refrain from moving. I'd been going

nowhere for too many years.

"Go home and write another one similar to that, and I'll put out a record on you," he said.

Our old car cruised at an altitude of 50,000 feet all the way home. But Val was not shocked when she listened to us babble the story like little kids.

"Carl, didn't I tell you God wouldn't let you down? Didn't I tell you He'd open the door? Thank Him! He's been awful good to us."

Within a couple of weeks I had written the song *Turn Around,* a love song for the flip side of *Movie Magg.* Released in early spring of 1955, it was collecting dust on the shelves of radio stations across the country by early summer. The same was true of our next record. I knew we would never have a hit recording ballads—they didn't show off our distinct sound. Mr. Phillips was aware of the problem, but he felt his company was too small to handle two boys, Elvis and I, with such similar styles. He felt we should continue singing ballads.

He had signed another distinct sound, Johnny Cash, so all three of us were booked on the same personal appearances. I stood backstage many times watching Elvis stir the audiences with "music with a beat," longing to throw my ballads away and join him. Within a few months Elvis was sold to RCA and the door had been opened. Mr. Phillips asked me to write some rock songs to record in the near future.

As I began doing more shows with Johnny Cash, I noticed certain qualities in the tall, lanky lad that set him apart. I became a fan for life when I first heard him sing songs he had dug out of his soul to uplift the hearts of poor and struggling common folk.

One night we were doing a show in Amory, Mississippi, when he said to me, "Carl, why don't you write a song and call it 'Blue Suede Shoes'?"

John had just returned from the Air Force where the boys had a saying while standing in line for chow: "Don't step on my blue suede shoes."

"That's a good idea," I replied, a little skeptical. A few nights later I was playing a club in Jackson when a very pretty girl was told by the fellow she was dancing with not to step on his blue suede shoes. The idea John had given me and the words of the boy connected. That night I couldn't sleep. About three in the morning I went downstairs and began picking away at "one for the money, two for the show, three to get ready, now go, man go! . . ." when Val called from upstairs, "Carl, whose song is that?"

"It's ours," I answered.

"I sure do like it. Finish it, Carl. It sounds like a hit."

I couldn't find writing paper, so I went to the kitchen, emptied a brown bag of potatoes, and wrote the words to *Blue Suede Shoes* on the bag.

One for the money, two for the show, three to get
ready, now go, man, go!
But don't you step on my blue suede shoes.
You can do anything–
But lay off of my blue suede shoes.
You can knock me down–
Step in my face and slander my name
all over the place.
Do anything that you wanna' do–
But uh-uh, Honey, lay off my shoes.

The song made me feel so good I wanted to shout, but the kids were sleeping. So I waited and called Mr. Phillips in the morning.

"Is it something like *O Dem Golden Slippers?*" he asked.

"No, it's about this fellow who don't want nobody steppin' on his shoes."

Mr. Phillips called us to Memphis in November, 1955, to record *Blue Suede Shoes,* and the song was a "take" on the first attempt. I was a little upset because I had made a mistake, saying the word "cat" instead of "man," but Mr. Phillips said we had cut a hit. He was right. *Blue Suede Shoes* was not only to become number one in country music, but also in pop, rhythm, and blues. No song had previously done that.

Although our release would soon be soaring to the top of the charts, it would be a while before royalty checks would come. It was Christmas, Val was pregnant again, and bills continued to monopolize our mail. We decided to spend the ten dollars we could squeeze from my pay on little Stan and Debbie. We bought Debbie a small doll and Stan a little red wagon. I knew the wagon was too small, but I had promised Santa would bring him one and that was what he was going to get.

On Christmas morning Stan ran towards his wagon, his eyes dancing with happiness. He sat down in it and over he went. He came running to us as the knot swelled on his head and tears rolled down his, Val's, and my cheeks. I sat there rocking my little boy who wouldn't go near the wagon and prayed, "God, please help me next year to buy Stan a wagon large enough for him."

The first few weeks *Blue Suede Shoes* was on the market it did very little; the local D.J.'s played the flip side, *Honey, Don't.* A month later I received a call from Mr. Phillips.

"Carl, you have a hit record. *Blue Suede Shoes* is sweeping the country like a storm. I just got an order for twenty-five thousand copies for Cleveland and the Chicago area."

I said, "Twenty-five hundred?"

"No, cat, twenty-five thousand!" he replied.

It was true! I finally had a hit record. Everyone was congratulating me on my success. Everyone but the people who ran the housing project where I lived. They called me into the office one day.

"Carl, we have been asked to have you move. You're behind in the rent."

"I'm not making any money, yet, but I will be soon," I replied.

Then she showed me the Memphis paper that said I was making twenty thousand a week from the record. She just wouldn't believe that I hadn't seen a cent of the royalties yet, so we had to find another place.

In two months *Blue Suede Shoes* peaked on the charts, and we were swamped with invitations for TV appearances. Our first was the "Ozark Jubilee" hosted by Red Foley, a kind gentleman I have admired all my life. Mr. Foley announced we would be making an appearance on the "Perry Como Show" the following week, the first time any country band would appear on national television. Although it was to be on another network and opposite Mr. Foley's show, he still gave us the plug.

The following Monday we played a show with Johnny Cash in Bono, Arkansas.

"You get 'em, King," he said, knowing how important the show was. He always called me "King" because he believed I was the tops in rockabilly music, the term for our musical style. The headlines in the local papers picked up on my success and prophesied, "From Bono to Como?"

Things were moving so fast I was dizzy with the excitement. I knew life had to go good now, real good. . . .

EVERY TIME I PASS A COTTON FIELD...

Even when I was knee-high to a grasshopper, I burned with a desire to make it big in music someday. My folks and relatives were all struggling sharecroppers, and as I grew older I couldn't understand their resignation to that type of life. I constantly dreamed of ways to relieve my family of poverty. And that dream never varied—I was always standing on stage at the "Grand Ole Opry" singing my heart out.

My first big chance at fame came too early for me to capitalize on it—I was in second grade. My teacher often began each day by leading the class in *Jesus Loves Me.* I don't remember the first time I heard the song, but I do remember those dark clouds, tornado winds, and heavy spring rains coming across the Mississippi River, pummeling the little shack we lived in. Because the land was so flat, the wind seemed to rip right across it, shaking the earth beneath our old wooden floor. Mama would call us all into the front room, and I can still hear her praying, "Lord, have mercy on us. Please don't let the storm blow us away." Then she would start singing *Jesus Loves Me,* we would join in, and peace would fill us as the storm roared on.

One morning as we were singing this song in school, the teacher said, "I hear someone singing mighty pretty." She listened a moment, then asked me to sing alone. I was scared. I had never sung in front of an audience before. But my love for the song overcame my fear.

A short time later, I was asked to sing before the student body in assembly. I can still hear the applause as I ended with ". . . the Bible tells me so." It was at that moment I knew what I wanted to be in life. I wanted to be a big-time singer. I wanted it with all my heart and soul.

Some time later our class was scheduled to put on a black-faced minstrel program in Ridgely, Tennessee, only a few miles down the road, and I was asked to sing *Oh, Susanna.* I ran all the way home excited. Mama got all excited, too, and borrowed ten dollars for some new clothes for me—and it wasn't even harvest time yet!

Every fall each of us boys got to pick out new clothes—a cotton shirt, a pair of jeans, socks, underwear, and shoes from the "wish book," a Sears catalog. It would take me half a day to make my decision. Then mama would send off the order, and as sure as the sun rose the following day, I would be impatiently waiting for the mailman. But I was always a little disappointed when the clothes finally came. What I saw in mama's old dresser mirror did not look quite like the model in the catalog. But the clothes had to last us until the next fall, so mama always ordered them a size larger than we were. Many times I stuffed paper in the toes of my shoes so I could walk.

I was so proud of my new clothes for the minstrel show that I wouldn't wear them on the bus ride to Ridgely for fear I'd muss them. It hurt me when Miss Loggins decided the ragged clothes I was wearing were better suited to the theme of the show. Reluctantly, I left my new clothes behind the stage and went to perform my song. When I returned, they had disappeared. Miss Loggins assured me I would get them back, but to a poor country boy, her promises seemed thin and of little comfort. I returned home broken-hearted.

Two weeks later Miss Loggins handed me a brown paper bag. Although they had been washed and the rusty water had turned my white shirt yellow, my returned clothes were beautiful! But just as important as the clothes was the kept promise.

About this time daddy contracted tuberculosis. The doctor said only rest and fresh air would cure him, so welfare became our only chance for survival. Often I would go with daddy to town to stand in line and receive free groceries—flour, dried milk, raisins, and prunes. At first I wasn't ashamed. But one day the teacher told me to wait at the end of the lunch line at school. After all the other kids had been served, I was asked to come to the counter. A tray was handed to me and I was told, "Carl, we know you are having a hard time at home so you don't have to pay for your lunch."

Then I realized that although everyone meant well, I was a charity case. I cried inside. Someday I would be the giver instead of the taker of charity!

Every time I pass a cotton field today and see whole families bent over in the hot sun I flinch a little. In order to keep from starving, my brothers, Jay, two years older than me, and Clayton, three years younger, daddy, and I had to work cotton from daylight to dusk, year after year. When daddy got sick, mama had to do it, too.

I can still hear daddy say, "Little Carlie, start at the bottom of the stock—like this, see? That way your little arms won't block the view of the cotton balls. You got to bend all the way down there anyways, so you might as well start at the bottom and work your way up."

"Yes, daddy."

"And don't you try to tote that old sack by yourself. Jay'll help you git it over to the weigh-in wagon."

"Yes, daddy." I was four years old when I started working, and I'll never forget—my sole desire that first day was to pick as much cotton as Jay. In order to get the white, fluffy balls out of the stock I had to get past the burrs, which I found difficult, so before long my hands were all cut up. But I didn't mind. The straw boss had given Jay and me a 9-foot sack, which we packed down as we went, and when it was filled, we toted it to the weigh-in wagon at the end of the field on the turn road. We had started at dawn, and before three hours had elapsed my hands had cramped and my spine was tied up in knots. After awhile daddy wanted me to quit, but I was proud even in those days; if Jay could keep going, so could I.

Meanwhile, all around us, the blacks were singing their spirituals—soul-felt messages in rhythm that stirred the emotions and greatly influenced my future composing.

I got shoes, you got shoes,
All God's children got shoes,
When I get to heab'n
Gonna put on my shoes,
Gonna walk all ober God's heab'n.

On Saturday when we'd get to town, someone would say to daddy, "Buck, which one of them boys pick so much cotton?"

"Little sized one right there," daddy would answer, pointing at me.

"Has he picked 300 pounds yet?"

"No, but he's gettin' close."

And one Friday afternoon, years later when I was eleven, I weighed my last draft for the day and it showed 302 pounds. I was so happy! I was dog tired. I could taste acid in my mouth. But I knew when daddy saw his best friends in town he'd say, "He made it." And they'd all know what he meant. I didn't stop to think that once daddy saw what I could do there would be many many days I would desperately pray, "Lord, please let the water outa that big ol' cloud. Let it rain so's we can get to rest." And every once in awhile He'd do it.

But working hard never made me bitter like I've seen some old boys turn out. I knew my penny a pound meant a whole heap to the folks. These were the Depression days of the thirties. Hunger humbled the biggest of men, took other men's lives who were less courageous. Flashy new cars came down our roads sometimes, perhaps looking for moonshine or a quiet place to escape the pressures of the times. Occasionally, the eyes of the rich met the eyes of the sharecropper and envy radiated from both sides as each desired something the other had.

We survived because of mama's faith in God and her ability to stretch those pennies we earned picking cotton. Candy was a rare luxury, but there was never a morning when hot biscuits and water gravy were not awaiting us for breakfast, or beans and boiled potatoes for dinner. Occasionally, mama would scrape up twenty-five cents for a pound of bologna, and we feasted. Where rich food, fine clothing, and warm shelter were lacking, love was abundant! Without a doubt, the foundation for my strong belief in God's love was laid in that three-room shack in Lake County, Tennessee. Mama reminded us constantly that Someone bigger and greater than any human earnestly cared for poor folks like us.

I knew that Someone surely cared for me the day Bildo came to live with us. Startled by the sudden scratching at the front door, I went to investigate. Looking worse than an overgrown rat after a swamp swim, a dog whimpered a pitiful cry as I opened the screen door. It was not uncommon for dogs to trade homes. Families who threw out more and better scraps usually had to contend with more stray dogs. But I became the happiest little boy in Tennessee the day that dog came to our house. To me he was more than an ugly little mutt; he was Bildo, my constant companion who listened to my every frustration. He could sense when I was feeling down, and he would pick those times to be the most playful, bringing a change in my life that everyone noticed. A large portion of my beans and boiled potatoes went to him every night, and when mama tucked us in, it was Jay, Clayton, me, and Bildo in one old bed.

Bildo had been with me for almost two years when one morning he started running in circles in the front yard, foaming at the mouth. Every time I tried to touch him, he would growl as if he intended to bite me. Mama came to the door. "Carl, get into the house. Bildo's sick," she shouted.

I ran to the house in tears. I looked out the window

and saw Daddy chasing Bildo with his shotgun. Mama tried to comfort me. "Carl, Bildo is going away. Jesus is going to take good care of him in his new home. Don't cry."

Then I heard the shot of the old 12-gauge, and a chill went up my spine.

Downhearted, Jay and I headed for the bayou to bury our friend. I was chosen to preach the service.

"God, do You hear me? Well, my name is Carl, and this here is my little ol' dog, Bildo. Daddy had to shoot him 'cause mama said he had some sort of rabies. Mama said You would take real good care of him, and I know You will, God. Now I don't know when I'll get to heaven, but remember he's my dog and don't give him to any other boy. You'll know him because he's the little brown dog that will follow You everywhere You go. Okay, God? I just wanted You to know I love him, and I thank You for watching after him until I get there. Amen."

The days were much longer after that. I tried to be brave and accept Bildo's death, but the question remained for months—why did Jesus have to take back my little ol' dog? Someday I'd ask Him.

BAYOU REUNION

The trip to the "Perry Como Show" in New York after *Blue Suede Shoes* hit was to be a long, hard drive. Because we had an interim performance in Norfolk, Virginia, we were forced to drive all night in a 1954 Chrysler limousine loaned to us by a Cadillac dealer in Memphis. Jay and I were in the back seat, Stewart Pinkhams was at the wheel, Clayton and W. S. were asleep in the front seat. It was about 6:30 A.M., and although we had only a few more miles to drive before one of us would relieve him, Stewart fell asleep. Our car hit an old pickup truck five miles from Dover, Delaware. Clayton, W. S., and Stewart were thrown from the car but received only minor cuts. W. S. found me lying face down in a pool of water and thought I was dead. He dragged me to a grassy bank. Jay was still in the car.

When I came to in the hospital someone was saying, "That's Carl Perkins lying over there. They say he's hurt bad. I hear one of them was killed."

I hollered for someone, and a nurse came running into the room.

"Who was killed in the accident? What happened? Tell me! I have to know!"

"Mr. Perkins, calm down. Your friends are fine, and you will be, too, if you remain quiet," she said, handing me a drink of water.

"But I heard them say one of the people in the accident was killed. Who was it? Are my brothers all right?"

"Mr. Perkins, please calm down. The person killed was the driver of the truck your car hit. Now please try to keep quiet."

I didn't believe her. I was in traction that evening when W. S. and Clayton came to see me. What a beautiful sight they were! But where was Jay?

"You better tell me the truth, boys. Is Jay dead?" I stammered.

"No, Carl," Clayton said, "Jay is not dead, and that's the truth. He was hurt a little worse than you. They took him to the hospital in Wilmington."

"What's wrong with him?" I demanded.

"His neck is broken, but the doctors say he'll be all right in a few weeks."

The days following were endless with pain, as I

recovered from a fractured skull, a broken shoulder, and multiple cuts and bruises. At the same time, I was plagued with doubts about Jay's true condition. I wanted to see him. I had to know he was alive. I begged the doctors to let me go to Wilmington. When they refused, saying it wasn't wise, I withdrew into depression. Now I was certain Jay had to be dead or they would let me see him.

Feeling I might not make a complete recovery if I did not see Jay, the doctors finally bundled me up and sent me in an ambulance to Wilmington.

They rolled me into Jay's room, and I cried when I saw him. He lay very still, but he was breathing. I asked them to put me right alongside him so he could see me when he opened his eyes. I lay there and waited. At first he was startled. He had thought I was the one killed! We were two happy kids once again sitting on the bayou together, although our hearts were filled with deep sorrow for the family of the truck driver.

At this time Val was far along in her third pregnancy, so the doctor advised her not to make the long trip to Wilmington to see me. I missed her dreadfully. Our room was filled with flowers sent by sympathetic fans, but it wasn't enough. I needed my girl. When they removed the traction, one of the hospital orderlies brought me his guitar. They opened the intercom to every room, and I sang *Blue Suede Shoes* lying on my back. The doctors said if I could sing that loud I could go home.

The following week Mr. Phillips called and asked me to come to Memphis. He met me with a wide smile. "Carl, it's good to see you. You look great. Come on, Cat, I have something for you to see."

We climbed into my worn-out car and drove to the Cadillac dealer down the street. Parked in front was the prettiest 1956 Fleetwood Cadillac you could imagine, and I pointed it out to Mr. Phillips.

"It's yours, Cat. Here are the keys," he smiled.

"What is this?" I stammered as a newsman began to snap pictures.

"It's for you," he answered. "I decided when I first got into this business that the first artist to sell a million records on my label would get a new Cadillac as a gift. By the way, what do you want me to do with your old car?"

I took the jack, old spare tire, and wrenches from the trunk, gave it a good kick for all the times it had failed to start, and said, "Mr. Phillips, do what you want to with it!"

When Val saw me drive up, her mouth dropped open; she got so excited she couldn't talk. It tickled me that for once she wasn't so cool and collected. We drove around half the night inspecting every inch of our beautiful chariot.

The booking agents were screaming at me to get back to work. There were new show dates coming in every day. Four important dates were coming up in Texas, and the bookers advised me to make them even if all I did was stand on the stage and sing *Blue Suede Shoes*. Our third baby was due any day and I did not want to leave Val, but we both decided I should fulfill my obligations.

On April 23, 1956, I was in San Antonio, Texas, with Johnny Cash when I learned Val had gone to the hospital. A phone was set up beside the stage, and I kept calling to check on Val. Just before I went on, the phone rang and I answered. When I walked out on the stage, I said, "Good evening, ladies and gentlemen. It's a boy!" Two days later I traveled home to my wife and new son, Stephen Allen Perkins.

After another month's rest Jay was able to return to the band, and once again the Perkins Brothers were making their own kind of music. We finally made the "Perry Como Show" a few weeks later, but the delay resulting from the accident caused a roadblock in my career. While my song was number one in the nation, I lay in a hospital bed as Elvis Presley performed it. But my country boy's dream had been partially realized. I had written a hit. The three dollars my folks had sacrificed years earlier to buy me a certain gift had finally paid off. That gift was a guitar.

One of the real joys of my childhood years was listening to the "Grand Ole Opry." Often we had to wait long periods of time before we could afford a new battery for the family radio, since we had no electricity in our home. But even though I enjoyed the Opry, something seemed to be lacking in the songs. Often I went to bed puzzled. One night, after a long day working the fields and listening to the blacks sing, I realized country music needed the black man's rhythm. I began to put that rhythm to every country song I learned.

Across the fields in a shack much like ours lived an old black man named John Westbrook. To me, he was Uncle John, and I could have loved him no more if he had been my real blood uncle. Every night I would beg dad to let me go listen to Uncle John sing and play his old worn-out guitar. He knew only three chords, but he taught me how to play those three well. I'll never forget his patience with me, his humble manner, and his deep faith. Many years later, inspired by his memory, I wrote a piece called *Uncle Ben*.

Mama and daddy knew how important music was becoming to me, so when Uncle John offered, they bought his old guitar for three dollars. I was so proud of it I wouldn't even play it. But soon my skinny fingers were aching as I tried to make new chords. I played along with Ernest Tubb and Roy Acuff on the radio, but always adding the black man's rhythm.

One day my teacher, Mrs. Lee McCutcheon, asked me if I wanted to play in the school band. I couldn't afford the white shirt and pants the band wore, so I refused. She must have known because she added quickly that the clothes would be provided.

I learned Miss Lee paid for the clothes herself; she even took my old guitar home and repaired the crack in the neck. Her big heart and radiant spirit really inspired me to try harder in everything.

Because we were determined to have a great band, we practiced almost every afternoon. One day Miss Lee told us we were going to perform on the number one station in the area, WTJS in Jackson, Tennessee, about eighty miles away. She asked me if I would sing *Home on the Range* as a solo. I had been listening to WTJS and often dreamed of performing on the radio. Here was my chance.

My heart started pounding when I saw the microphone. It seemed unbelievable—all I had to do was sing into that thing and folks would hear me for miles. After the band played a couple of songs, a big, burly man motioned me down to center stage. I took a deep breath and belted out *Home on the Range* as I had never done before. I think I even startled myself.

As we were leaving the station, I heard two men talking. "That little fella can really win an audience. He didn't just sing words. He sung meaning into that old song." Did they really mean me? No one else had sung a solo. I knew then God must have heard all those prayers I had been praying recently.

Not many yards behind our home lay a graveyard. At its rear was an area secluded by shrubs and vines. It was here I established my first radio station. I took a Pet Milk can and nailed it to a broom handle, stuck it down into the dirt, and that was my microphone. All that next summer when I was not working, I was singing once again on WTJS! Jay and Clayton were the audience. They played their roles well and often requested that I sing their favorites. I hardly realized I was developing a style—I was just putting a beat to country tunes.

Things were getting harder at home. We had moved from our three-room shack to an old one-room storehouse. Mama hung a sheet for a partition. Our stove was an old tin barrel dad set upon some bricks and placed in the middle of the floor. It kept us from freezing that winter.

One very cold morning I walked into my school classroom and saw a box of clothing sitting beside Miss Lee's desk. The other kids were placing clothing in the box, and I thought it strange no one had said anything to me about bringing clothes. After school Miss Lee asked me to stay for a few minutes. I was worried that I had done something wrong.

"Carl, your classmates don't feel sorry for you. They just love you and want you to stay in school this winter. Now help me take this box to the car, and I'll drive you home."

As we toted the box to the car, the little bit of embarrassment I felt was eclipsed by my friends' love for me. I found clothes in the box for Jay and Clayton also. One of the prizes I discovered was a pair of corduroy knickers. I put those knickers on, but my socks didn't reach them. That mattered little as I strutted to school in high fashion.

I won't mention the boy's name, but he is one person I will never forget. One day the following spring, we squared off for our usual football game. He and I were on opposite sides, and I was playing in the backfield. Well, here he came, running over every boy on the field. He was coming right at me, and my mind was tugging my soul in two. Should I tackle the boy whose pants I wore or should I let him score? Making my decision, I took a flying leap at his legs and brought him down.

"If you tackle me that way again, I'll take my pants back," he snapped.

That hurt. "Someday, buddy, I won't have to wear yours or anyone else's pants," I yelled. "I'll practice my guitar until I'm good enough to get on the 'Grand Ole Opry.' I'll show you what I can do."

I always figured I owed that old boy something because he had fanned my fire to succeed. Later in life that "something" was a new mohair suit tailored especially for him from me.

As in most homes, Christmas was a special time for

us. Though Santa could not afford much for poor kids like us, we knew mama would convince him to drop off a few oranges and peppermint sticks. Dad, Jay, Clayton, and I always went to the woods at Christmas and chopped down the prettiest evergreen. Mama would string little red holly berries and popcorn until our tree was magnificent! But mice shared our home, and often we awoke to find the popcorn gone.

One Christmas, mama decided to wrap up raisins we had received from welfare to give to our friends as gifts. There were only enough raisins for a few, so I chose my closest friends. But that Christmas I received thirty-three gifts from my classmates and Miss Lee. I'll never forget how I felt not being able to give them gifts.

I remember the day Pearl Harbor was bombed. I was in the fourth grade, and Miss Lee told us to not be afraid. She said we should all pray silently for God to help us. I did not know what a Pearl Harbor was. I reasoned it must be the place where the country kept all its pearls, like Fort Knox where all the gold was. I sat in my seat with my head bowed asking God to forgive the Japanese people for bombing Pearl Harbor and stealing all our pearls.

After school that day I went to my grandfather's house.

"Pappy, why do those Japanese people have to go and steal our pearls?"

He just laughed and explained to me that they had not stolen a thing.

"Carlie, they are just mad with us."

"Well, what are we gonna do?"

"I guess we will have to fight," he murmured.

"You mean fight like war?"

"I'm afraid I do, son," Pappy replied.

I did not understand war. I believed then, and still

do, that instead of everyone having a fight involving everybody, why not let the two or three at the top who disagree fight it out.

Reelfoot Lake is a famous resort area located outside the town where I lived. During the war, sailors from the nearby naval base went there to relax. Taking my guitar, I would go there and get up on a picnic table and pick and sing. They always tried to give me nickels and dimes, but I wouldn't accept. I felt sorry for them. Many times I would get home and find a dollar bill tucked in my guitar somewhere.

Often I was leery of people who tried to help. I felt their friendship was generated by pity, so for years I allowed only my family or cousins to be my best friends. Although we were scattered over the countryside, we cousins found ways of getting together either in the fields or at the school we all attended.

One afternoon when I was in the fifth grade, an assembly was called. Jay, Clay, and I along with two of our cousins, Billy and Donald, met in the gym to sit together. Donald had a pocketful of marbles, and naturally we were all more concerned with playing marbles than listening to the speaker. Donald threw a handful of marbles across the floor, disrupting the whole auditorium, not to mention the two teachers who almost slid into the gym wall. I knew we were in for it. After the assembly, Mr. Thomas, the principal, asked all five of us to meet him in his office. We decided we would not tell who did it. But more than the principal's paddle, I dreaded mama and daddy finding out—they would be hurt.

Mr. Thomas sat at his desk. Much to my surprise there was no paddle in sight.

"Well, boys, what do you have to say for your conduct? Who threw those marbles?" he asked.

We looked at each other and were silent.

"I want to know which one of you threw those marbles?" he repeated.

Still not a word.

"If that's the way you want it, then you will all suffer the consequences," he said, pulling the paddle out.

I swallowed hard.

"Mr. Thomas," I managed to say, "we decided that we would not tell you which one of us threw them marbles, because you see, sir, we Perkins stick together. We don't want no whuppin', but we done wrong. We're awful sorry we threw them marbles, and we promise we won't do such as that again. You can go ahead and whup us if you want to, but will you promise us one thing?"

"What's that?" he asked.

"Us boys ain't never been in no trouble before, and there ain't no one ever had to whup us except our parents, and they'd feel mighty bad if they knew. My daddy ain't been well for a long time, and he'd be hurt the most of all. See, he thinks we act like young men, and he's so proud of us. Please don't tell nobody you whupped us!"

Mr. Thomas did not speak. He just kept looking down.

"Boys," he said after a pause, "I am not going to whip you, and I promise I will not tell a soul you had to come to my office. You just be the young men your dad thinks you are."

We left his office, and although he had not whipped us, his attitude had served a far better purpose. Never again were any of the Perkins called into that office.

Jay, Clay, and I would often gather pecans and sell them in town. We loved to go to the picture show, and that was one sure way of earning the money. When I heard that a famous entertainer was appearing in person at the Strand Theater on Saturday—Tex Ritter, my idol—I wanted to go so desperately. I had never seen a famous person. But we hadn't been able to sell enough pecans. I felt the world had once again slighted me because I was poor.

Years later when I was on tour with Tex Ritter, I related this story to him. Sure enough, he remembered the Strand Theater date because of the great fish dinner he was served afterwards. He told me he wished he had known about the country boy who cried himself to sleep because he could not see the Tex Ritter Show.

What I did not know was that soon I would meet the *most famous* man in America. School was dismissed early one afternoon because there was to be a parade in honor of the president of the United States, Harry Truman. Everyone started pushing as the president came our way and many hands reached out to him. Suddenly, I found I was not only standing beside the president of the United States—my foot was definitely planted on his. Then he was staring me right in the eye.

"Hello, son. How are you?" he asked, patting me on the head.

I could not speak. Quickly I removed my foot. He passed on through the crowd, and my heart followed him. I was certainly one happy little boy. For the first time in my life I felt fate had dealt me a lucky hand.

A half mile down the road from our house lived a little black boy named Charlie. We worked together in the fields, we played together in the afternoon, and he was the first to teach me a lesson about life—that a man cannot be an island.

Every morning I would meet Charlie at the big oak tree to wait for our buses. Mine was always first, but one morning his came early—a big truck with a bunch of laughing, black kids in the back.

"See you after school," he smiled as he climbed in. I was shocked! It hurt me to see my best friend climb aboard a worn-out truck while I boarded a fairly new bus. I never understood why there had to be such differences. Charlie and I were equal in God's eyes, but we certainly were not in man's.

On Saturday we would go to the show together, but when we arrived, Charlie was told to go to the balcony and keep quiet. I sat in my front-row seat, wondering if Charlie could even hear what was going on. I would have sat in the balcony with Charlie, but that was not allowed because he was black and I was white. Charlie never once complained. He just humbly accepted his life and made the most of it.

I wish I could have foreseen how much better my life might have been in later years had I let more of Charlie's humility and patience rub off on me. I was going to have a long, hard struggle for acceptance, too—in the entertainment world.

A NEW LIFE, A NEW SOUND

I was fourteen years old when mama and daddy announced we were moving to Bemis, Tennessee. They felt the opportunities in a small cotton-mill town were greater than in sharecropping, but I knew I would miss the serenity of the cotton fields. I loved to get off by myself and practice my guitar under a shade tree or just daydream after work.

Dad's brothers had secured jobs for minimum wages in the mill, but he was turned down because of his lungs. Greatly disappointed, we were once again forced into sharecropping with a local landowner. Life seemed a little kinder to us this time, though. The soil was richer and our living conditions were far better. We lived in a well-built house, had electricity for the first time, and even a refrigerator. What a thrill it was to listen to the radio often without fearing the battery would go dead!

I was happier than I had ever been. As life began smiling at me, I began smiling back. But I was needed more and more in the fields. My teacher, Mrs. Kirby McKnight, tried to discourage me from quitting school.

"Carl, your education is the most important thing in your life right now." But I had made up my mind. In the spring I quit, never to return. At times I have regretted it. But who knows—if I had remained in school and pursued another career, I might never have realized my life's dream of writing and singing songs that would give folks happiness.

The next year we moved to Mrs. Patton's place where the land was supposedly a bit richer. Dad would always say, "The blacker the soil the better the crops, boys." And we did realize a small profit that year.

I was riding a cultivator headed back to the fields one day after lunch when Clayton wheeled by on his bicycle. The bicycle scared the mules, and they broke into a gallop. I fell from the cultivator, getting tangled in the plan lines, and mom, dad, and Jay riding behind in a wagon watched helplessly as the mules dragged me fiercely for a half mile. When the mules were stopped by a barbed wire fence, I freed myself from the lines. I was cut and bruised all over and my clothes were in shreds. But I was alive! I lay for two days without the services of a doctor, but the Great Physician watched over me and I was soon back in the fields.

My childhood dream of becoming a "Grand Ole Opry" star became more and more an obsession. I practiced my guitar every spare moment, always encouraged by mama. Jay would sit and listen, too, so one day I said to him, "Jay, why don't you learn rhythm so we can play together?"

"I bet I can't make one chord," he said. But Jay found he could, and the two of us spent hours practicing.

One day, dad heard that a dairy farmer was looking for a family to move onto his farm to help him with his business. It was in the early fall and most of our cotton still lay in the fields, but dad was eager. Mr. Day needed a man and a boy to help with the milking and delivery. Dad felt this was our big chance to get free of our sharecropper's cross.

"Now, boys, Mr. Day is offering us a fine opportunity, but we won't go unless you all want to. I know none of you ever spent a night away from home and none of you will probably want to, but if you decide to do it, one of you has to go now."

We looked at one another, and the old Perkins spirit was stronger than ever.

"Sure, dad, we'll go," Jay said, as we nodded our heads.

But then there was a silence. I knew Jay was too shy to leave home and Clayton was too young, so it was up to me.

"Daddy, I'll go up to Malesus and live with Mr. Day," I said.

"Okay, son," he replied. "I'm mighty proud of all of you."

Jay looked over at me, and his eyes told me how grateful he was. The following Monday I said my good-bys as cheerfully as I could. Mama handed me the brown paper sack of extra clothes and off I went. As I walked, I cried. I didn't know what lay ahead. I hated leaving my family, but I knew I had to face it like a man!

I was nervous and timid around Mr. Day and his wife, though they were warm folks. We sat down to supper that first night, and before me was the biggest piece of meat I had ever seen. I had lived seventeen years and had never seen a T-bone steak. I ate a few of the peas and potatoes, waiting to see what Mr. Day did with his meat. He cut off a small piece and ate it. My eyes widened. That whole piece of meat on my plate was all mine! I dug in. I didn't know you weren't supposed to try and cut across the bone, and the steak flew off my plate sending little peas all over the table and onto the floor. My face reddened. But I just picked that steak up and tried again!

That winter our family was together again, but getting up at two in the morning to milk Mr. Day's sixty-five cows in severe cold became too much for dad. His health began failing, and so we moved to a three-room house in town.

Jay fell in love with a young lady, Pauline Helton, and married her. He moved out, leaving me as sole supporter of mom, dad, and Clayton. Jay was making twenty-five dollars a week at a mattress factory, so I decided to join him. To me twenty-five dollars was a lot of money, but it didn't go far in feeding, clothing, and sheltering four people. Of course, Clayton worked, but he did not feel the need to give mama and daddy what he made.

Jay and I still found time to practice our guitars. Clayton purchased a bass fiddle and began to practice with us. Before long we became known as the Perkins Brothers' Band with the Carl Perkins' beat! If we were good, we were not satisfied; we had to get better. We entered a talent show in Malesus and tried hard to excite the audience with our style. The applause didn't let up for minutes! They gave us the best band award and I won best vocalist.

But daddy's health continued to deteriorate; his lungs were very weak because of the many attacks of pneumonia. One night he became so ill we called Doc Smith.

"Carl, I can't do a lot for your father," he said, after examining dad. "He's weakening with each passing hour. If he lives through the night, it will only be because God is merciful. If you could get him to the Baptist Hospital in Memphis, he might make it."

"Doc, we're poor folk. How do I go about getting him in that hospital?"

"About the only way I know is to talk to the welfare people in Jackson," he replied.

Daddy lived through the night, and I knew I had to get him to that hospital. Early that morning I went to the welfare office. The woman listened sympathetically but told me the hospital was filled. Then God must have worked a miracle, because in a few minutes she returned and said Memphis would accept daddy. That evening we laid daddy in the back of my uncle's 1941 car and headed there. I'd never driven in that large city and I was scared.

The hospital was so full that daddy's bed was put in the hallway, but he received good care. The doctor told us the only way daddy could survive was to have the infected part of his lung removed. Mama told him to do whatever he could to save daddy. Twenty-one days later we brought him home. He was never able to do any difficult work after his recovery, but he was alive.

Daddy's recovery forced me to acknowledge that God was still around. I never doubted that He was a merciful God who cared, but my life wasn't centered on Him. It was centered on our family's needs. There had to be an answer that would free us from poverty. Someplace, someday I'd find it—and maybe more of God, too.

SOUL ON FIRE

It was April of 1949. My cousin Martha and I had been to the post office and were cruising around town in my old '34 Ford coupe. She'd just been telling me about a certain girl she was sure I'd enjoy getting to know.

Martha was the sister I was never lucky enough to have. I had a deep respect for her opinion on anything, especially my music. When I was twelve and wrote my first song, *Movie Magg,* she said, "Carl, that's real good. You oughta write some more. Did you write that all by yourself?"

Through the years she continued to help and encourage me—she had a gift for learning lyrics quickly.

Now, as we drove down Main Street, she suddenly grabbed my arm. "Carl, there's the girl I've been telling you about. Let's stop and give her a ride."

One of the prettiest girls I had ever seen stepped into my old rattletrap. She had beautiful red hair. Martha introduced her as Valda Crider. I don't remember saying much, but I do remember the little-boy feeling I had when I looked at her. We took her home, and when she got out I asked Martha, "You reckon she'd go out with me sometime?"

"I think she just might. Do you want me to ask her?"

I assured her I did.

The next day I was at Martha's house when she came in from school, grinning. "She said she'd go. She thinks you're real nice looking. I told her you'll treat her good," Martha said with a "you better" look as she handed me Valda's phone number.

I called her as soon as I got home and asked her to go to the drive-in that coming Friday night. I borrowed my Uncle Ernest's car and put on an extra splash of vanilla flavoring, the poor boy's cologne. But when we drove into the drive-in—it was Val, Martha, and I. I sat there all through the show listening to their giggling, and I decided then Val was going to be my girl.

Our dates were limited to weekends because of my heavy work load. Sometimes I grew depressed thinking about my still unfulfilled dream of a career in music, but then I'd think of my red-haired gal and things would be better. We had our disagreements, but there was a deep love growing between us. I knew Val would become my wife.

However, I was still needed to support my family. Many times I almost asked Val to marry me but didn't, knowing it would mean hardship for my folks. Finally in 1953 things got easier, and I asked her to spend the rest of her life with me. I told her there was no way we could have our own place right off, that we'd have to move in with mom and dad.

"Carl, I understand," she said. "One day we'll have a place of our own."

It wasn't much of a wedding and there wasn't a honeymoon. We were married on Saturday, and I had to work the next day at the Colonial Bakery. Mama found a job in a candy factory in Jackson and Val went to work, too, easing my load.

The week following our marriage, I was laid off. While I looked for work during the day, I played two or three nights a week in the clubs around Jackson. Now that I needed it most, I couldn't find work. But perhaps if I had gotten into a trade or something steady I never would have taken the side jobs in the clubs and gotten the experience that eventually led to the realization of my dream. However, when I learned Val was pregnant, I really wondered how we were going to make it.

On September 17, 1953, Val woke me about five in the morning. "Carl, I think this is it. Get me to the hospital, honey."

I was so tired from playing till two that morning I said, "You can't be having the baby. You're two months early. Go back to sleep. Everything will be all right."

A little later I was woken again by Val's tugging. "Carl, get up! We've got to get to the hospital."

I jumped up, alarmed now, and drove her to the Jackson General Hospital. They wheeled her down the hall, and I took my seat beside the other "fathers to be."

Why was the baby coming so early? Something was dreadfully wrong.

"God, please," I cried, "don't let anything happen to Val or our baby."

For ten hours I prayed and paced. Finally, as I was standing with my nose pressed against the glass of the maternity ward door, I saw a nurse come toward me with a bundle in her arms. But the face of the critter inside was too red, the head too long.

"Whose baby is that?" I anxiously asked.

"It's the Perkins boy," she replied with a smile.

I almost fainted. I was a daddy! Each day when I visited Val and saw him behind that plate glass, I prayed, "Lord, please help me be the father to little Stan that You'd have me to be. And help me, Lord, to give him some of the things in life I never had."

The next months were probably the most financially difficult I have ever known. Val did ironing for her mother and sisters; I picked cotton during the day and continued playing guitar at night. We had moved to a little apartment of our own and our rent was only $32.50 a month, but there were times I wondered if we would make it. Many a night I walked to Yate's Grocery to get milk on credit for our baby. On top of that, Val announced she was pregnant again! God knew how hard it was to support one child; I had to believe He would help me somehow to provide for another. "But, Lord," I prayed, "if You could see fit, could we have us a little girl baby this time?"

Debra Joye Perkins was born November 9, 1954.

The winter of '54 was quite severe, and many a night I fought through bad weather to play in some honky-tonk for a meager two or three dollars. Discouragement plagued me constantly, but Val never lost faith.

"Carl, we'll make it. I know God hears our prayers, and He has never let us down. Wait and see—one day you'll write that song that will change our lives. Just keep trying and be a little more patient."

But it was difficult to believe with her when I couldn't get the things she and the kids needed so badly. I guess I didn't realize God had already given me everything important without my earning it.

The booze was free at most places I played, and it eased the pressure. My intentions seemed good. I wanted to try and help the drunks, give them some happiness, maybe a little hope. But I was in the devil's playground, and it wasn't long before some old boy would shout, "Give that Carl another drink and he'll really pick and sing."

I would mix the beer with the whiskey and, with soul on fire, I'd stand on table tops, striving for the attention I thought my music deserved. Though the club work helped feed my kids, the way some of them operated bothered me. The chances of a customer leaving with half the money he came in with were slim. Many of the waitresses were hustlers who could easily maneuver a man to overspend. While a girl danced with him, another would bring his half-empty bottle to my brothers and me. I'd put it in my amplifier for our night's use. If the man realized what was happening and put up a beef because he had to buy again, he was escorted quickly to the door. I know now it should have bothered me more because it was stealing, and I was part of it.

More and more I was failing to support my family as an entertainer. I had known from the beginning the road would be rough, but I wasn't prepared for it being this bad. I remembered Charlie and his willingness to sit in the balcony—I knew I had to keep doing my best and not get impatient—there had to be a break coming from somewhere. I couldn't turn my back on my music. It was all I knew. It was all I'd ever wanted to do, rough or not.

I had no idea that soon the mercy of God I had seen in my family through the years was about to work on my behalf.

HE'S PLAYING A GOLDEN GUITAR

Jay, Clayton, W. S., and I continued playing our hearts out, accepting every booking, driving long hours to play in some backwoods dive for little pay.

But then came that miraculous day in 1955 when I heard Elvis Presley on the radio and tore off to Sun Records, which led to Johnny Cash asking me to write a song about somebody's blue suede shoes which changed everything.

After all the years of hurting, hoping, and praying, it felt good to hear my songs being played over the air, to be called "King" by the man I loved and respected—and to be able to walk into a store and buy things without even checking my wallet because I knew it was plumb full of greenbacks.

For the next several years the Perkins clan rode the tidal wave of success, appearing on TV, doing concerts, and yes, finally even the "Grand Ole Opry." I was especially glad for my brothers—they'd stuck with me through all the hard times—even if they didn't spend their money too wisely after we hit it. I guess none of us did, for that matter.

It was while we were doing a tour of the northern midwestern states in late January, 1958, that I noticed Jay didn't smile once during the show, and his usual masterful technique was off. The following morning I went to his room. He was reading the paper.

"How you feeling', ol' buddy?" I asked him.

"Fine," he answered.

"You sure? I noticed you missed a few last night."

He looked up at me quickly, then turned away. "Yeah, I know. I promise I'll do better tonight."

"What's the problem?" I asked, getting concerned.

He didn't answer right off. Then he said, "It's my left hand. It keeps going to sleep. But it's looser today."

"It's probably just this cold northern weather you're not used to. You'll be all right when we get back down home," I said.

"Sure. Let's go get breakfast."

He got up from the bed and almost fell to the floor.

"Jay, what is it?" I asked, grabbing him.

After a moment he said, "Carl, my left side keeps givin' way and tingles a lot."

"You're going to see a doctor right now."

"No, Carl, he'll only put me in the hospital."

"Well, then, you're going home and see a doctor, and I mean today."

"What about the tour?"

"The tour isn't as important as your health."

That afternoon I had tears in my eyes as I watched Jay board the plane. He had to be all right. Maybe he was just pushing too hard.

A few days later I returned home to find Jay worse. He was rapidly losing the use of his left side. The doctors in Jackson suggested he go to a hospital in Nashville. They felt he had pressure on the brain but didn't know why. Curiously enough, the doctors in Nashville diagnosed his problem as a severe nervous disorder. They said the immobility of his left side would continue until he freed himself of stress.

"Something is causing you to be unusually nervous," the doctor said. "I suggest you find out what it is and get rid of it. If it's your guitar, slide it under the bed and never play it again."

Jay tried to relax at home, but distressing headaches interrupted. Back at the hospital in Jackson, Dr. Tyor, a brain surgeon who visited the hospital every other week, emphatically disagreed with the Nashville doctors.

"Jay's trouble is associated with his brain. He may be suffering from some mild nerve disorder, but that's not what's causing his severe headaches and trouble in his left side. I advise you to enter him in the Methodist Hospital in Memphis for further tests."

Jay underwent a number of tests, and days went by without any announced results. I caught Dr. Tyor in the hall a week later.

"Carl, as of this time we have localized the problem to the brain stem. We know there is pressure on his brain in the form of a blood clot or tumor. Only exploratory surgery will tell us which it is."

I had never heard of exploratory surgery. "Will he be well after you do this?"

"I cannot give you the answer now. Exploratory surgery allows us to diagnose so we can prescribe treatment."

I grew apprehensive. The operation was described as very delicate; one slip of the scalpel and Jay could be left without his vision, his hearing, or both. Two hours after Jay had been taken to the operating room, my nerves bordered the breaking point. I escaped from the waiting room to find some comfort in being alone in Jay's hospital room. I was sitting there with my head bowed—not praying, not even thinking, just waiting—when an orderly wheeled Jay in. Still asleep, Jay looked pale and pitiful with his head bound in bandages.

I looked at the brother I loved so and remembered our growing-up years back on the bayou. I remembered my first day of school and Jay's words, "Carl, now don't you be scared. You ain't got no reason to worry. Most of the kids your age can't even write their names. But look at you. You already know how to write it, you can count to a hundred, and you even know two and two makes four." He took me to my class, and when he turned to walk down the corridor a lump came to my throat.

But Jay would always meet me at lunchtime to give me my share of biscuits and fatback mom had packed for us.

And he never failed to ask, "Carl, did you get good marks today?"

When I answered that I had, he'd smile and say, "See, Carl, I told you you could do it." His words were all it took to inspire me to do my best.

A couple of years later when Jay walked down the aisle in church to give his life to Christ, I wanted to, too, but didn't. I remember the tears of joy that streamed down my parents' faces. Jay began to walk down a new road of life seeking to live for Jesus rather than himself. He sought freedom from human faults, a freedom that could only be found in God. But I couldn't understand why Jay had to tell everyone that he was a believer. Why, everyone could tell he believed by the way he acted. One day I asked him why he had walked that aisle.

He just smiled and said, "One day you will do it, too, Carl. Mama told me God expects us to tell the world we love Him, and that's what I did. One of these Sundays you'll get the urge to do it and nothing will stop you. Now, don't you worry. It will happen." And, just like that, confusion was defeated by Jay's heartwarming words. He had a way of overcoming life's heartaches, especially the heartache of being poor. When we'd sit and look at the "wish book" and I'd pick out the expensive things, Jay would say, "Carl, what you wanna go and do that for? You know mama and daddy can't afford to buy them things for you."

I would always answer, "Jay, we ain't gonna get nothin no way, so why not wish for the best. You gotta want big things or else you'll never get anything."

Jay would never argue. He tried to convince me arguing was a waste of time and energy. To me it was a sign of courage. One had to face disagreements with facts and force. I admired him for his self-control, a characteristic that had always evaded me.

He never worried about riches or desired anything beyond his power to attain, like I did. I was always going off by myself to daydream. Someday I would be rich and famous I told the crows, the sun, and the crawling things that inhabited the banks of the bayou.

But now that I had accomplished most of my dream, there was still the big "wish" for Jay. Here I was climbing the golden stairs, while my brother, who was richer in spirit perhaps than any of us, was sinking somewhere inside the mystery of unconsciousness. Something was not adding up right, and I wanted to argue with someone about it—even God.

After the surgery the doctor said, "Carl, your brother has a malignant tumor on his brain stem. I removed as much as I could, but the tumor is located in a delicate region. I'll prescribe something to relieve the pain."

I had never heard of a malignant tumor, but I figured the medicine Dr. Tyor would give Jay would dissolve it in time. I walked into the waiting room and told my family.

As we were walking to the car, Val asked, "Carl, do you know what a malignant tumor is?"

"No, not really. I'm just glad Jay is going to be okay."

She stopped in the middle of the parking lot.

"Carl, it's cancer."

"What?" I asked incredulously.

"Carl, a malignant tumor means cancer."

My knees weakened. Although "malignant" was not a part of my vocabulary, "cancer" was. Cancer meant death. I had to talk to the doctor. There was a phone booth at the rear of the parking lot.

"Yes, Carl, I'm afraid Jay has, at most, a year to live," the doctor said. "I advise you to take him to the Baptist Hospital for cobalt treatments. They will slow down the growth rate of the cells, but they won't kill all the cancer. I'm sorry."

I hung up the phone and went to Val, broken-hearted. Jay was dying, and there was nothing I could do.

"Carl, God's will is often difficult to accept, but you have to try," Val said, holding me. "I love you, and I'll be beside you every step of the way."

Val and I decided it would be better if we kept the

bad news from my family for awhile. And Jay was never to know. Was it best? Maybe so, maybe not. However, I knew Jay would suffer more knowing others were burdened for him.

A month later we brought him home. He had lost twenty-five pounds, but he was still Jay. He never spoke of his pain, although often the morphine didn't help. Beads of sweat would appear on his brow, but he would smile and say, "Carl, you know I feel pretty good today."

After a couple of months he was able to get out of the house for short periods of time. Often we would invite Jay's family to our house for supper. He had to be helped from the car to the house and always brought a little pail. One night I found out why. He was eating some of Val's famous spaghetti when suddenly he jumped up and headed for the bathroom with his pail so he would not make a mess. He grew weaker each day. All I could do to help was pay his bills and give him a small check each week.

Johnny Cash came to see Jay often, lifting his spirits with humor. I will always be thankful to John for loving and caring for my brother so keenly. A month before Jay's death, John suggested we take him fishing since Jay had been an avid fisherman all his life. John, Clayton, W. S., Marshal, Luther, and I all went.

For a few hours Jay was a boy again sitting on the bayou, dangling his toes in the cool water, watching Clayton land a prize—a big turtle.

And then only a few days later I received a phone call at three in the morning.

"Carl, get over here right away. Jay's acting awful funny," Clayton cried.

We had been taking turns sitting up with Jay, and this was my night to sleep. I found Jay semi-conscious. The family was gathered around. I knew it was just about over.

"Don't you be scared," he whispered, calling each of us by name. "I know I'm dying, but I'll be through with all the suffering soon. I know where I'm going. It's just over the hill. Hear 'em singing?" And he drifted into a coma.

Four days later I was sitting at his side with the family when he opened his eyes, looked deep into mine, moved his mouth as if he were trying to speak, squeezed my hand, and died.

The next few days held little meaning, even though everyone was so kind to all of us. A month after Jay's death, Johnny Cash called me to say he had spearheaded a big show to be produced in Memphis as a memorial fund for Jay's family. Every big country entertainer in the business either appeared or sent a telegram. I stood backstage, tears streaming, listening to Ernest Tubb, Jay's idol, sing the songs I had often listened to Jay sing.

The following months were extremely difficult. Many times I would go to the old pond where we had fished, and it seemed I could hear Jay say, "Carl, move over to the other side. They're biting there!" And sure as shootin', I would catch a fish.

I turned away from God completely. How could the God I believed in take my brother in his twenty-ninth year? I needed Jay. He had been my right-arm brother. I did not want to think about it. I just wanted something to help me get through the day. I began drinking heavily again. But in spite of myself I thought of God often. At times I hated Him for the frustrations of my life; at times great surges of love for Him would pour out of me, and I would grab a piece of paper and write and write—poems, songs, recitations. Most I discarded, but this is part of one song that I kept.

This morning when you woke up
Yesterday had vanished–it was gone.

And, my friend, today you're one day closer
To the day you'll have to move along.

Yesterday is gone forever
And there is no need in crying ever
Put a smile on your face
And on your lips place a song
Because today you're one day closer
To the day that God will call
And you'll go home
Oh, yes–yes, you are.

I was watching the "Rifleman" one night on TV, a series about a widow man who tried to raise his son the best he could. I started wondering what it would be like raising my little old boys without Val, and before I knew it I was reaching for some paper to write *Twenty-one.*

One day I got a phone call from the governor of Louisiana, Jimmy Davis. I had never met him but always admired songs he wrote like *You Are My Sunshine* and others.

"Carl," he said, "I heard about a song you wrote called *Twenty-one.* It sounds like something I'd love to hear. What are you doing today?"

"Nothing really," I answered.

"How about playing it for me? I'll send my jet down to pick you up."

I spent two days with him, and it was good because I'd been feeling down. His wife was sick, and he had me go to her in the bedroom and play *Twenty-one* for her. Big tears flowed down her cheeks as I sang.

Twenty-one, Boy, twenty-one
Now you was just a young fellow, Son,
The night your poor mama died.
You don't remember it now, Boy, but we was both by mama's side.

DISCIPLE IN BLUE SUEDE SHOES

You see your ma had this sickness, Son
From all the hard work she'd done
And she prayed all of her life
That God would let her raise you to be twenty-one.

Me and you never moved into town, Boy,
We just kept living out here.
Things have been pretty tough for the past
twenty-one years.
I remember now when you was a little fellow
I used to take my boy to church.
I'd see you in the choir with them other younguns,
And it gave dad's heart a jerk.
Why you sounded like a little angel, Boy,
And to papa you sure did look sweet,
Even though your little ragged britches
Came half-way to your skinny little knees.

And when the service was over
It filled your papa's heart with joy,
Preacher would step down and pat your little head
and say
"Carl, you got yourself a fine little boy."

Me and you would get into the old wagon, Son,
You'd look over towards dad and smile,
I'd hand you the lines and let you drive the team a
little while.

Yeah, life's been tough for me and for you, too, Son,
And you know I guess I've prayed all of my life that
I could raise you to be twenty-one.
So tonight maybe my life down here is about over,
Boy,
Maybe my work on earth is about done,
Maybe now I'll get to go see the Lord and live with
your mama again, Boy,
Cuz tonight my baby's twenty-one.

Jimmy Davis liked it so much he recorded it, since he's quite a performer himself. To this day I receive a little royalty from it.

Another song I wrote that year was *Walk With Your Neighbor* which was recorded by a folk singer from Canada, and it became quite popular in that country.

The next year I wrote two other songs that for some reason I never discarded. Folks often called me Cotton Top when I was young, and one day I was reminiscing about my early days and this song came to me:

I want to tell ya'll a story
About the flat black cotton country
Called Lake County, Tennessee.
My story's about a little skinny-armed,
Underfed country boy named Cotton Top
Raised in a land so poor that if
You was on welfare
You was looked up to.

This little feller had one old busted guitar
One string, but one soul full of determination.
Kids used to come by and they'd say,
"Hit your lick, Cotton Top!"
He'd go . . . (instrumental fill)

Well, they must've fallen from the sky,
I don't know where, but
One day Cotton Top came up with
Two more strings.
That made him three,
Kinda changed his sound,
But his beat stayed the same.
He went kinda like this, then,
He went . . . .

DISCIPLE IN BLUE SUEDE SHOES

Then one Christmas Eve, Cotton Top's dad
Came home with a brown bag,
And in that little bag was
A set of slick, long, shiny, steel
Guitar strings.
That kinda changed his sound again,
But that beat stayed the same.
People come around and said,
"Hit your lick, Cotton Top!"
He'd go . . . .

Well, the beat got around,
And then one day
They called him to Carnegie Hall.
A forty-piece band had to step aside,
When the golden curtain opened wide
There sat Cotton Top with a smile.
Somebody in the balcony hollered,
"Hit your lick, Cotton Top!"
He went . . . .

Yeah, little Cotton Top picked,
And the whole crowd knew
He'd make it to the top
With the chosen few.
When you're in New York
Just bummin' around,
Step inside the Hall
And listen for this sound,
'Cause embedded in the walls
Forever to stay
Is the sound of a little skinny-armed,
Underfed boy named Cotton Top.
That goes to prove
With only one string
And one soul full of determination
And one land like America
You can make it,
Yeah, you can make it.

Now, play, Cotton
Play, boy! . . .

Cotton Top!

The other song was inspired by an extraordinary lady we called Aunt Ruth. Her yard backed up to mama's, and one day I was sitting and looking out in the yard when Aunt Ruth came out and nimbly hung her wash. It was surprising to me because she was blind. I knew I had to talk to her.

"Aunt Ruth, how are you?" I asked, approaching her.

She tilted her head at me and smiled, "Oh fine, Carl, ain't this a beautiful day?"

"Yes, it is," I answered. "But it's much prettier now 'cause you said that. But tell me, is it beautiful because it's warm out or because you hear those birds singing so pretty?"

"Oh, yes, there's beauty all around me."

"I'd like to ask you a personal question, Aunt Ruth. Do you ever feel cheated because you're blind?"

"No, Carl, I don't feel cheated," she answered without hesitating. "You see, the next thing I'm going to see is God. That's what I look forward to."

When I was home again, the words just seemed to be piled up wanting to come out. I grabbed a pencil stub and wrote:

One day I stopped, I talked with a blind man, and
he said these things to me. . . .

I really don't mind being a blind man
For God is the next thing I'll see.
My ears hear the sounds of the water flowing down
to the creek below,

And my hands touch the trees, God put them here for me
'Cause He loved me so.
So, I really don't mind being a blind man
For God is the next thing I'll see.

And he said,
Mister, it's true I can't see the sunset like you can
But you know something, sometime the clouds might cover up your sky
And I'll keep seeing my pretty sunsets just the same
'Cause, see, I don't look at it with my eyes.
But I know there's beauty out there 'cause I can hear it in the songs the little birds sing to me
So, Mister, do you understand, you really don't have to have eyes to see.

'Cause my ears hear the sounds of the water flowing down to the creek below,
And my hands touch the trees, God put them here for me
'Cause He loved me so.
And I really don't mind being a blind man
For God is the next thing I'll see.

Writing seemed to help my inner turmoil some, but it couldn't solve my problems or help me control my drinking. If I suspected God held the answers, I didn't act like it. I bent my knee to the devil in rebellion, and in return he broke my body and almost destroyed my soul.

ANYTHING YOU SAY, DEVIL

The devil chased me with alcohol for about eight years. During those years I lived in hell, tormented daily by addiction and the knowledge of what I was doing to those I loved most. Alcohol ripped through my life like a howling tornado, leaving ruin in its wake, forcing those whose lives it touched to reach down deep into their souls for inner strength. I lost my identity and self-respect and at times became overwhelmingly paranoid. I was Satan's slave without any hope of ever regaining my freedom.

The Bible says we reap what we sow in life. Each time I escaped trivial worries by drinking I was giving Satan more control. Today I realize the Bible is true when it calls him a murderer. He tried to murder me gradually by poisoning me with his brew, or by getting me so drunk it was dangerous for me to drive or perform—like the time when I was drunk and stuck my hand through an open fan on stage and almost died.

The only good thing about my experience with alcohol was that I learned Satan's ways. I know he lusts for souls. That's why so many youth today are doing drugs and perishing from overdoses or bad dope; that's why there are ten million alcoholics in the country.

The Bible says there's a spiritual war going on constantly—and it's over the souls of men. First the devil will try to kill a man to keep him from following God. If he fails here, he'll try to stop the Christian from being effective for God any way possible—even causing death. Recently, I have become aware of the thousands of Christians who die prematurely through disease.

Perhaps you drink a little alcohol but boast that it will never become your god. That's what I said when I took my first drink at eighteen. It began slowly and then picked up speed at an uncontrollable rate. I cannot stress too strongly the horrors I lived through. I'd wake up in the morning with sharp pains in my head, a sick stomach, full of remorse for something I'd done under the influence, and apprehensive about what I'd have to face that day. That's usually when the evil one would first speak to me. Working through my thoughts, he'd say, *Carl, you're scared, aren't you? One drink is all you need to ease the worry and eliminate the physical pain, too.*

I'd reach around for a bottle, only to find it empty. And then panic would set in. How could I make it without a drink? My hands would start shaking. *Carl, you've got to have a drink. Get up! There's a bottle under the car seat left from last night.*

I would go get it, and after one swallow my hands were steady, courage filled my soul. In a little while the effect would wear off. *Now what are you going to do? You can't get through the rest of the day without a drink.*

I remember one morning I reached into my pocket and found my last ten-dollar bill left from the previous night's pay. I didn't want to spend it when the kids needed so many things. I put it back into my pocket, disgusted that I was still as poor as ever.

Carl, it's rough, I know. You have had it rough all your life. You can't help the way you are. The kids won't go hungry. Val will see to it. Now take that ten dollars and purchase a big bottle. I tried to fight back, but, as usual, I lost. I headed for the door.

"Carl, why don't you stay here with us and forget about getting another drink? I'm so afraid you might have an accident," Val would plead.

But nothing mattered except that drink. Even if I had to physically get her out of the way, I'd do it. And when I'd be getting in the car my little old boy's voice would still be ringing in my head. "Daddy, don't drink any more. Stay at home today with us. Maybe we can go fishing like you promised. Please, daddy."

At the tavern I'd meet someone I knew, start drinking, and slip into a numbing euphoria that soothed my nerves; soon, I loved everyone in the world. At two o'clock in the morning the owner would drag me out to my car and point me home. Many times I narrowly missed telephone poles or parked cars. Police cruising the streets never noticed. Shrubs lined my driveway, but

I never hit one of them. I would stagger into bed, leaving my clothes strewn across the floor. In bed I'd make promises to myself and God. And the next morning it would begin all over again.

On January 15, 1959, Val once again gave me a child. The day Jay died she had told me, "Carl, I know how much Jay meant to you, and I'm praying this baby will be a boy. You can name him after Jay to keep his precious memory alive." I was deeply touched because I knew how much Val wanted another daughter. The birth of our fourth child was difficult. Val's life was in jeopardy throughout the delivery. I sat in the waiting room torturing myself, believing God was punishing me for having served the god of the bottle.

"Oh, God, please be merciful. Don't take Val or the baby. I know I've done wrong, but I will try. Please don't take either one of them like You did my brother Jay."

A calm voice interrupted my prayer. "Mr. Perkins, you have a new baby boy and your wife is doing fine."

"God, I'm so ashamed. Thank You for sparing Val and giving me a son. I am going to be a better man with Your help. I promise!"

I stood before the window watching little Gregory Jay Perkins crying. Often it is hard to believe God is so good, and as I stood there I could only bow my head in humility.

"Carl, I don't know how she pulled through this one," the doctor said. "But I do know another birth will probably kill her. You are a lucky man! No more pregnancies!"

I knew God pulled Val through. I knew it then, but I didn't remember it when the devil called me back to the bottle.

Months slipped into years. My career came to a standstill because I had lost my desire to pursue my country boy's dream. Again I turned from God. Instead of reaching up and filling my heart with His strength, I reached down and filled it with booze. Memories of the days when I was a recording star, surrounded by my brothers, clouded my thinking. I had gone from a rock 'n roll king to a helpless nobody. I worked only when there was no money for food for my family or—more important—booze for me.

Photo by Gravemann

"Mama and Daddy knew how important music was becoming to me, so when Uncle John offered, they bought his old guitar for three dollars. I was so proud of it" (p. 42).

"One day my teacher asked me if I wanted to play in the school band . . . she even took my old guitar home and repaired the crack in the neck. Her big heart and radiant spirit really inspired me to try harder in everything" (p. 42).

(Carl playing guitar in band -- 4th grade)

"Jay and I still found time to practice our guitars. Clayton purchased a bass fiddle and began to practice with us. Before long we became known as the Perkins Brothers' Band" (p. 54).

(Jay, Carl, and Clayton Perkins)

"My cousin Martha introduced me to one of the prettiest girls I had ever seen, Valda Crider" (chap. 7).
(Val and Martha)

"I encouraged W.S. Holland to learn drums... when he finally joined us, our sound had the added impact of percussion" (p. 20).
(Carl, Jay, W.S., Clayton)

"Johnny Cash, Elvis Presley, and I were booked on the same personal appearances. I stood backstage many times watching Elvis stir the audiences with 'music with a beat,' longing to throw my ballads away and join him" (p.22).

(Carl and Elvis sign autographs)

Photo by Gravemann

"Sometimes I grew depressed thinking about my still unfulfilled dream of a career in music, but then I'd think of my red-haired Val and things would be better" (p.58). (Carl and Val)

reamed of being on
Grand Ole Opry,'
we had not convinced
ne important that
ad it" (p.19).
(Carl at the White House)

"Dad was liked by everyone. He transmitted sparks of love through laughter" (p. 115).
(Carl and His father, shortly before His father's death)

Photo by J. Phillips
The Nashville Tennessean

"I was a member of Johnny Cash's show for nearly a decade. I know now it was God's plan . . . I will always claim John as my third brother" (Chap. 12).
(José Feliciano, Johnny, Carl)

WELCOME, KING OF ROCK N' ROLL!

Early in 1963, "Lucky" Moeller, a special friend and owner of a booking agency in Nashville, called me. "Carl, there's an agency in London that wants you to do a tour there with Chuck Berry. The money is good, and, Carl, you need to get out of this rut you're in. This could be a real opportunity for you. Why don't you talk it over with Val and call me back?"

"Carl, that sounds like an answer from heaven to me," Val said.

"Val, I don't know. You know how nervous I am. I don't think I can."

"There you go again with that defeatist attitude. Sure you can't, if you believe you can't. I believe you can, and I say try, Carl, just try."

"You really believe I can do it, don't you?"

"I sure do, and I know you can be a big success if you will leave your bottle here."

Two weeks later I boarded a small plane in Jackson, the first leg of my trip to London, without my bottle. I was scared. What had I gotten myself into? I arrived in Memphis, just eighty miles from Jackson, and my nerves were already shot. I had to have one drink. I passed a bar in the airport only to return for one electrifying drink. I knew if I did not eat I would be tempted by drinking on the plane, so I ate and ate. I arrived in London sober and had gained confidence. The bookers met me at the airport and took me to the hotel. On the way I gawked at all the sights I had so often read and heard about. I could not believe I was actually in London, England, being driven to my hotel in a limousine!

Alone in my hotel room, I began to fidget. The devil reminded me of the bar downstairs, but I opened my window to the sounds of the night to drown out his voice. I had promised Val I wouldn't drink. I could perform without it! If I failed too badly, I could go home. No one knew me here. I dressed for the show, continually talking to myself out loud, blocking the devil's voice.

And then I was backstage and listening to the roar from the audience as the announcer said, "I give you the King of Rock 'n Roll, Carl Perkins!"

I walked on stage and was met by many signs saying, "Welcome, King of Rock 'n Roll." The applause was long and vigorous. Tears filled my eyes as I felt love and appreciation from them. I performed with a vitality I had never felt before. The standing ovation at the end of the show was just too much to handle. I could only bow in gratitude. I could feel God's presence in that moment, His strength seemed to be all around me.

But alone again in my room that night I was unstable as my nerves began to rebound from the excitement of the evening. Again the devil taunted me with the bar downstairs—that one drink that would magically calm me.

But my earlier victory before the show gave me strength to say "no" again. And God was the reason. He was showing me He had not deserted me—and never had through the years. To help me further, He gave me the idea to call Val right then. She was so happy. "Carl, you keep trying and I'll keep praying. God loves us!" she cried.

The tour lasted four weeks, and during that time I never once got drunk. I was experiencing a rendezvous with God each time I walked on the stage. For the first time since Jay's death, I felt there was still a place for me in music. I performed each night to the best of my ability as new energy continually filled me. I nearly jumped through the stage many nights from pure excitement.

After the last show the promoter asked me if I would like to attend a party. We drove for about two hours through London and its beautiful surrounding countryside.

"Where is this party?" I asked, wondering if he was indeed taking me to a party.

"Just a little further, Carl," he laughed and turned the car into a driveway marked by willow trees.

Up ahead I could see what appeared to be a castle.

"You sure this is the place?"

"Yes, Carl, this is the place."

DISCIPLE IN BLUE SUEDE SHOES

We walked up to the front door, and a waiter dressed in white gloves and long-tailed coat answered the bell and asked in precise English, "May I say who is calling, sir?"

"Carl Perkins," Mr. Arden replied.

I looked at Mr. Arden and laughed out loud. "My name won't get us into a place like this."

After a brief moment the gentleman returned. "Right this way, sir."

We walked through a magnificent hallway and into a huge ballroom filled with well-dressed people.

"Mr. Arden, that fellow standing over by the table looks like Ringo Starr, one of the Beatles," I said, staring.

Ringo spotted us. "Hey, fellows, Carl Perkins is here!"

Eyes turned to me, and four fellows walked toward me—the renowned Beatles. I was speechless. They informed me that the party was in my honor. I met other famous people like Roddy McDowell, who I had always admired. Someone brought in a guitar and I sat on the couch, with the Beatles sitting around me on the floor. At their request, I sang every song I had ever recorded. They knew each one. I was deeply flattered when George asked, "Hey, Carl, how did you kick off *Movie Magg*?

I showed him, and he jumped up and yelled, "See, boys, I told you we didn't do it right!"

I continued singing until I had sung every song I knew. It was three in the morning when the party was finally drawing to an end. As I was leaving, Ringo asked, "Carl, what are you doing tomorrow night?"

I had planned to go home, but I didn't mention this.

"We are recording tomorrow night," he said, "If you'll come, we'll send our car for you. We'd be honored!"

They would be honored! "Sure, fellows, I'd love to."

I returned to my hotel, still floating on clouds of disbelief. I had to call Val again. "Honey, they want me to come to their recording session. It looks like I'll be a day or so late getting home!"

"Honey, I'm so happy for you. You stay as long as you need to. Something good is about to happen to you. I love you."

The next night I sat waiting in the lobby when a chauffeur told the desk clerk he had come for Mr. Perkins. I jumped up and said, "Yes, I'm Mr. Perkins."

He escorted me to the Mercedes limousine, and I sat in the back seat of that big car as people stared at us motoring through London.

How lucky can one man be? I asked myself. *Here I am on my way to hear the number one group in the world record.*

At the studio the Beatles were tuning up. Ringo came over to me and asked, "Mr. Perkins, do you mind if I record one of your songs?"

"Do I mind? Man, I'd be grateful!" I said, knowing what this could mean to me financially and in many other ways. He turned to the others and shouted, "He doesn't care if I record his songs!"

That night they recorded three of my songs: *Matchbox, Honey Don't,* and *Everybody's Trying to Be My Baby.* *Matchbox* was released as a single, and they were all included in the "Beatles '65" album.

The next morning I sat in a big jet headed across the Atlantic Ocean, a changed man. I had been blessed by God, and I was grateful. I will be forever thankful to the Beatles and to the fans in England for restoring my faith in my music and for helping me see God more clearly.

At home things were better. There was money to catch up on bills. I started going to church with my family. I took my boys fishing. I left whiskey alone. Val had been right. I had been able to do it.

UNLESS A SEED DIE...

In the latter part of 1963 I was asked by the governor of Tennessee to do a few shows in support of his reelection. I finished up early one Saturday so a friend asked me to accompany him to a club in Dyersburg, Tennessee, to hear a band performing there. I still wasn't walking totally on God's highway—I had started drinking again and, this night I had a few in me and was raring to go.

Naturally, I soon found myself on the stage singing the old favorites. The crowd was hot. They were applauding wildly and I was taking my bow, throwing my left arm behind me like always—when I jammed my hand into a large unprotected fan.

There was a horrible sound of bones being crushed as the blades tore through ligaments and tendons. People were screaming as blood pumped from my mangled hand. Someone threw a towel around it, and I was rushed to the Dyersburg hospital.

Because the hand was so mutilated, they advised me to get to Jackson to see a bone specialist. By now the pain was excruciating. Lying in the back seat of my car, I sweated and gasped for air. The blood kept flowing from the wound, and I could feel my strength leaving. Toward the end of the seventy-five-mile trip I slipped into shock. I was dying. A loud banging noise brought me around. The motor had locked up! The highway patrolmen, escorting us, put me in the back of their car and continued the trip.

At the hospital I remember hearing Val scream, "He's dead! Tell me the truth. He's dead, isn't he?" Then I passed out again.

I was given five pints of blood before they operated. Dr. Barnett, a bone specialist, told Val he would have to amputate two fingers, at least.

"Doctor, I know Carl will be able to use them again. Please don't amputate. How will he play his guitar? Please try to save them!"

Three-and-a-half hours later I was returned to my room with all five fingers intact. With God's help Dr. Barnett had performed a miracle.

The next day I awoke to find Val sitting at my side. Oh, what joy to be alive!

"Val, how bad is it? They had to take some of my

fingers off, didn't they?" I asked.

"No, you still have all your fingers, thanks to the Lord."

My hand was numb. I couldn't believe I had all my fingers. A cast covered my hand except for the thumb and reached all the way to my elbow.

Later the doctor said, "I did the best I could do, but I'm afraid it might not have been enough. I doubt if you'll use that hand for playing again."

I closed my eyes and cried. I knew I was reaping what I had sowed.

For six weeks I waited, wondering if the hand would be usable. The uncertainty nearly drove me crazy. I needed help, and again I turned to whiskey. The day the cast was removed I saw a beautiful sight. My fingers were actually there, though the last two were stiff and without feeling. I knew that somehow, some way, I would play my guitar again. "Thank You, God," I sighed, softly.

The next weeks were filled with pain, but I was determined. I kept squeezing a rubber ball until I slowly regained use of my fingers. The little one remained crooked and numb, but it amazed me that it was bent so that it easily wrapped around the neck of a guitar. "A double thank-You, God."

That winter I stayed pretty close to home, working my hand through chords, forcing the little finger to stretch out, and soon I was doing pretty well with it. I even accepted some bookings.

On April 9, 1964—my thirty-fourth birthday—a couple of buddies asked me to go rabbit hunting.

"Will you be late for supper?" Val asked as I strapped on my boots.

"No, babe, I'll be in around six. Now don't you worry about me. I'll be careful, and there will be no booze for me today!"

DISCIPLE IN BLUE SUEDE SHOES

As I drove to pick up Jimmy and Pete, I felt the beauty of a wonderful new day reaching out to touch me. I was happy to be alive and sober.

"Pete, you reckon those rabbits could smell us coming and left these woods?" I chuckled as we trucked through mud up to our ankles.

"I've got a little something here that'll make you see those little rascals even if they ain't there," Jimmy said, holding out a bottle.

"No thanks, Jim. I promised Val I wouldn't drink today," I said.

"Oh, Carl, one little drink never hurt nobody."

Suddenly, I was very thirsty. I grabbed the bottle. "Well, here's to all the rabbits that got away."

There was still no sign of rabbits as we tramped along drinking and carrying on like sixteen-year-olds.

I looked at my watch. "Hey, boys, it's 6:15 and Val was expecting me at 6:00! Guess we better get on home!"

"What time do you think we ought to leave tonight?" Pete asked. Pete and Jimmy were going to ride with me to Cleveland where I had to perform.

"Well, it's a good ten-hour drive to Cleveland. We better leave by midnight if we want to get there in time for me to do the show. Can you be ready?"

"Sure. Just come by the club a little before midnight."

We sped home, and my conscience tore at me for breaking my promise to Val. Why did I have to take that first drink? Couldn't I have had a good time without it?

When I pulled the car into my driveway it was 7:30. I walked in like a little whipped pup.

"Carl, I was so worried about you. Why were you so late? Oh, it doesn't matter. You're home safe, and that's all that counts," Val said planting a kiss on my cheek.

Either I had put on a good show or she was catching

a cold and couldn't smell the liquor.

"What time are you planning to leave tonight?" she asked.

"About midnight."

"Why don't you try to get some sleep? It's a long drive."

I had consumed just enough alcohol to make me want to do anything but sleep. I wanted another drink. I finally got dressed and left about 11:30. I reached under the car seat and found the bottle of liquor left from the hunting trip, and by the time I arrived at the club where Pete worked, I was flying high. Pete was counting the money taken in for that night.

"Carl, have a seat. I'll be through here in a minute," he yelled from behind the bar.

The front door swung open, and two policemen came in. One of them was a rookie, and I could smell trouble as he glared down at me.

"Don't you know this place is closed for business?"

"Sure, I know it's closed, but I am not here to party. I was just waiting for Pete to lock up so we could be on our way."

"The best thing you can do, mister, is to get on home. You've been drinking, and it's after midnight."

My temper began to burn. Who was he to order me to get out? I was about to tell him exactly what I was thinking, when Pete, suspecting what was about to happen, rushed over to the table.

"Officers, I need to lock the doors. We have a show date to drive to, okay?"

"Okay, Pete. Just make sure this drunk doesn't drive."

That did it! I wanted to knock his head off. Who was he to label me a drunk? I wasn't drunk. That badge was no protection for his smart-aleck tongue. Pete hastened them out the door.

DISCIPLE IN BLUE SUEDE SHOES

We picked Jim up and headed for Cleveland, and Jim wanted to drive first.

Soon a siren sounded, and Jim pulled over. Two policemen came to the car, and one was the same cop I had confronted earlier.

"Officer, was I speeding?" asked Jim sheepishly.

"Yes, buddy, you were!"

"We're on our way to Cleveland. There's no traffic. Guess I pushed the accelerator a little too hard."

"Okay, we'll let it pass this time. Just take it a bit slower."

He was turning away when his partner spotted me.

"Hold it! Just a minute! What are you still doing out?" he asked me.

"He told you. We're on our way to Cleveland. I have to perform there tomorrow," I answered.

"Okay, fellas, out of the car," the policeman ordered.

They searched the car and found my half-empty bottle under the seat and my hunting rifle in the trunk.

"Whose car is this?" the officer asked.

"Mine," I said.

"Okay, Mr. Perkins, you're under arrest."

He read me my rights and shoved me into the patrol car.

"Why are you taking me to jail?" I asked. "What have I done?"

"For starters, Mr. Perkins, you were carrying a concealed weapon."

"I forgot to take the gun from the trunk after a hunting trip today."

"Tell that to the sergeant."

Bang! The cell door closed. All night I sat, thinking. How could I have gotten to this point—to be caged up like an animal? Instead of admitting that alcohol had caused me to break the law by carrying an opened bottle and being careless with a weapon, I tried to blame it all on the cop, society, and even God.

"Yes, You! God," I said aloud. "What have I done to deserve this? You know the bookers will slap a lawsuit on me for missing the Cleveland date! How will I provide for my family now? We needed that money! You caused this to happen! Are You really the great God, the performer of miracles of love? Then why this?"

I lay on the cot seething in anger for quite a while. But toward morning, deep within my heart a calm voice spoke.

Carl, don't be afraid. I have not turned My back on you. This happened for the best. Tomorrow you will be released from jail. I love you. I brought you to this to show you just how much I do love you. I will lead you out of darkness and will provide for you forever. Do not let your soul be troubled. Trust in Me, My son. Have I ever failed you? Remember, there's no one on earth who loves you as much as I do.

My heart was lifted to the heights. Would I be given a second chance to prove my love for Him? Deep, peaceful sleep came to me. The next day I was released, but with a brand-new attitude.

Val and I purchased a little farm about thirty-five miles from Jackson with the royalties we received from the Beatle records. Mama was still working in the candy factory, and her health was poor. Dad's had stabilized but wasn't good, either. So early in 1965, I moved my parents to the small farm and told them, "You'll never have to move again. Your next address will be heaven."

I visited mama and daddy often, enjoying the sweet serenity of the fields. What a warm feeling I got watching my folks grow healthier each day!

One morning when I was fishing and looking up at a pretty blue sky, a thought came to me. America was fixing to go to the moon, and daddy and most folks believed we'd never succeed. They felt if God had wanted men to fly that high he would have built rockets into their backsides. Well, I didn't know about that, but as I looked up at that sky I thought, *Wouldn't it be sad if man got carried away and put a big old black hole in that pretty sky?* But I knew that man would get to the moon sooner or later, and as I sat there fishing this song took shape in my mind.

Well, there never was a mountain that he couldn't climb,
And there's never been a treasure that he couldn't somehow find.
They couldn't hold him down even though they tried,
They said his airplane would never fly,
They said he'd never make his car roll across the land,
But if anybody could, Buddy,
A man can.

They laughed when Columbus said the world was round,
They said the ocean would glurp him right down,
But he proved they were square when he found the land,
And if anybody could do it,
A man can.

I guess Columbus wondered what in the world for,
'Cause the land he found was soon at war.
They couldn't get along over the color of skin,
And if anybody could start one, I guess,
A man can.

Why, he's cheated his neighbor.
He's killed his fellowman,
Starved his babies, took his own life in his hands.
And God sent His own son so we'd know love true.

Then man saw fit to kill Him, too
How anybody could kill his Savior, I cannot understand,
But if anybody could fool you,
Boy, a man sure can.

He wasn't satisfied till he reached the moon,
And he may be reachin' now for his final doom.
I cannot help but wonder, yeah, I do wonder why
Does man really want to put a hole in God's beautiful sky?
There's a lot about us creatures I don't understand,
But if anybody can confuse you,
A man can.

You look around the world, and you too will wonder why
Little children go hungry, get sick, and die,
When we could all know happiness and we could have peace in our land.
But if anybody can stop it,
Just watch it . . .
A man can.

That fall, my friend Tony Moore and I decided to go squirrel hunting on the farm. Tony had begun playing drums for me and didn't drink. He tried to convince me I shouldn't either, and there were times when his words worked. We had been out a couple of hours when I leaned my gun against the fence I was about to climb through. Suddenly the gun fell, firing. Buckshot struck my left ankle. Tony rushed me to the Jackson Hospital where Dr. Crocker told me he would have to amputate my foot.

"Doctor, I know you can save his foot," Val pleaded.

Three hours later the operation was over and my foot was wired to my leg.

DISCIPLE IN BLUE SUEDE SHOES

"Carl, you still have your foot, but let me warn you—you may be a cripple. You may drag it a little when you walk," the doctor said.

I endured another six long weeks of waiting until the cast was removed. During that time I prayed to God I would be able to walk. And with His help I walk today as well as I did before the accident. I experience swelling and numbness occasionally, but it's a good reminder of the period in my life when I was running from the Master.

I was becoming more and more aware of God's power, and I was growing scared. It seemed He was always right behind me and wasn't giving up. I was bothered daily by His love shining through His people, but I was convinced I had no right to ask for forgiveness. I didn't realize He had already forgiven every sin I had ever committed because of what Jesus did for me on the cross. All I needed to do was let Him have those sins.

On Easter Sunday in 1966 I made that public commitment of my life to Christ I told you about earlier. I got out my cotton sack, packed it down tight with a whole lifetime of sin, and toted it down to Jesus' weigh-in wagon at the turn road. Oh, how good it felt to get that heavy burden off my back!

I didn't know what to expect next, but just as He promised, I became aware of His guidance daily. Life didn't suddenly become a bed of roses. But a great consolation to me was that He had promised to lead me through this life and on to a far better one in the end.

Yea, though I walk through the valley of the shadow of death,
I will fear no evil:
For thou art with me;
Thy rod and thy staff they comfort me.
Thou preparest a table before me in the presence of

mine enemies:
Thou anointest my head with oil;
My cup runneth over.
Surely goodness and mercy shall follow me all the days of my life:
And I will dwell in the house of the Lord for ever.

Psalm 23:4-6

GOD SENDS A MAN IN BLACK

I opened the door one day in January, 1967, to find Johnny Cash standing on the other side. It was wonderful to see him again, but I was saddened to see how thin he was and to learn he had become as hooked on drugs as I was on alcohol.

"Carl, why don't you come to Atlanta with us?" he urged. "We've got to do a couple of days there. It would be like old times. Come on and go with us."

That was the beginning of perhaps one of the closest friendships any two men have ever shared. After the Atlanta dates, John asked me to become a regular on his road show. Val and I talked it over and decided it could be beneficial to both John and me in many ways.

I hobnobbed with some of the finest folks in the music industry while with John. The Tennessee Three—Marshall Grant, Luther Perkins (no relation to me), and W. S. Holland were a constant inspiration to me. None of them drank, and they spent many long hours trying to convince me I didn't have to, either. If I needed someone to talk to, even at 1:00 A.M., all I had to do was call. Often, all three would show up.

And how can words express my feelings for those four fine young men, the Statler Brothers? They quickly became "brothers" to me and constantly gave me encouragement. Harold Reid, one of the Statlers, is famous for his humor. I can remember standing backstage many times with the jitters before a show. Then Harold would tell a joke, and we'd all roar and become more relaxed. The Statler Brothers had a mystical power of love that blessed me each time I was around them.

The Carter Family: June, Anita, Helen, and their mother, Maybelle Carter, were also members of Johnny's show. I have admired this great family all my life and felt it a real privilege to work with such talent. I have never known a sweeter, more inspiring lady than Mother Maybelle Carter.

Yes, these are the folks who helped me the most by their love—the ones who said, "Carl, don't give up. Don't start drinking again. Keep believing in God!"

I was a member of Johnny's show for nearly a decade. On that cold, January day in 1967 I did not know why Johnny Cash once again entered my life. I know now it was God's plan. I needed the change Johnny's show brought—especially the love and inspiration of my brothers and sisters in Christ. How I thank God for them!

In August of 1968, Luther Perkins, John's guitar player, was killed in a tragic fire at his home. It was a sad loss. Luther had great talent, and he made a unique sound on guitar.

"John, I can't play like Luther, but I'll be glad to stand in his place," I said.

And for the following six months I stood in Luther's place on stage, but I never once took his place as the famous lead guitar player on the Johnny Cash Show. Bob Wootten, a talented musician from Nashville, was later hired to replace Luther.

Our tours usually lasted ten to twelve days a month. They were often hard and fast, but they were rewarding. One day in 1968 while we were traveling in the Midwest, I was sitting in the dressing room playing my guitar and letting my mind wander out loud.

I remember when I was a lad,
Times were hard and things were bad;
But there's a silver lining behind every cloud.
Just poor people that's all we were
Try'n to make a livin' out of black land dirt;
We'd get together in a family circle singin' loud.
Daddy sang bass, mama sang tenor,
Me and little brother would join right in there. . . .

Harold Reid said, "Carl, that sounds like a good song. You oughta write that one down."

With Harold's encouragement, I scrambled through my guitar case, found an old piece of paper, and wrote the words down just as I felt God was giving them to me. Johnny came by and heard me.

Singin' seems to help a troubled soul.
One of these days, and it won't be long,
I'll rejoin them in a song;
I'm gonna join the fam'ly circle at the throne.
No, the circle won't be broken,
Bye and bye, Lord, bye and bye. . . .

"King, whose song is that? I sure do like it!" John exclaimed.

"Well, it's mine. I've just written it."

"Sing it for me all the way through."

After I finished, John told me he wanted to record it, and I was honored. After the tour we went to the Columbia Studio in Nashville and John recorded *Daddy Sang Bass.* The song quickly became number one in country music and in 1969 was nominated by the Country Music Association for the "Song of the Year" award. My royalty, at one cent per record, came to about $150,000, thanks to Johnny Cash!

Through the days of his inner battle with the devil and eventual victory, I have watched the "Man in Black" come alive. I believe that in his own way he is becoming one of the great preachers of our time. He doesn't claim to be a minister, but wherever he goes he leaves folks thinking about their relationship with God. He's not satisfied with knowing a little about the Bible; he wants to know all he can. He studies it and tries to live accordingly. He may be unpredictable, whether it's eating steak with his hands while dining with the queen or shedding a tear at the sight of a hungry dog, but he does what he feels is right.

No one thought religious songs would go over in the "Showroom" of the Hilton Hotel in Las Vegas, but Cash proved them wrong.

When John got back from filming *Gospel Road* in the Holy Land, I learned we were booked in the Hilton Hotel Easter week. I thought it strange because that week was usually "off" time for our group. And then I learned he planned to show the film there and had selected that week for greatest impact. Frankly, I was concerned. I felt there was a strong possibility the audience would walk out. His manager, the critics, everyone told him, "John, you can't put that screen up in the biggest club in Las Vegas and show pictures of Christ toting that cross." But Johnny Cash isn't afraid to be a fool for Christ. He even went to Nicky Hilton and asked that alcohol not be served while the show was on, and Hilton agreed.

The program was tastefully done. John showed scenes from *Gospel Road,* and we sang appropriate songs. In one scene, Jesus was playing with children on a beach, and we sang *Children, Go Where I Send Thee.* We sang *Follow Me* for the scene where Jesus dealt with Mary Magdalene. There were times in between songs when John "rapped" to the audience—"This is something June and I have felt compelled to do. One night June had a dream. She saw me standing on a mountaintop with a Bible in my hand, talking to millions of people about Jesus. Later, when the idea of a film came, I knew I had to tell the story of Christ the way I felt about it."

The last scene was of Jesus hanging on the cross, with the casinos of Las Vegas in the background. John just bowed and walked off the stage. It was electrifying. Three thousand people rose to their feet.

From the cotton fields of Dyess, Arkansas, Johnny Cash has risen to super fame because he is not his own man—he is the Lord's! And I will always claim him as my third brother.

BLUE SUEDES TURN GOLD

God seized every inch of my soul after I willingly cast my bottle into the Pacific Ocean that day in 1967. Though I had turned from God's love after I had become a Christian, He took me back. And even today if I backslide, God is always there to rescue me. In His Word God says:

> *But if from thence thou shalt seek the Lord thy God, thou*

> *shalt find him, if thou seek him with all thy heart and with all thy soul. When thou art in tribulation, and all these things are come upon thee, even in the latter days, if thou turn to the Lord thy God, and shalt be obedient unto his voice . . . he will not forsake thee. . . (Deut. 4:29-31).*

How thankful I am that God continued to love me and gave me another chance to show love to Him. My life took on a new dimension after that day on the beach. I found my forecast to be correct—I had to take one day at a time and commit each new one to Him. The devil continued hurling temptation at me, but every time I asked God to help, rather than depending entirely on my own power, He did. I'm proud to say that I've never taken a drink since that day on the beach ten years ago.

I began praying to be used to further His kingdom, and in 1969 He led Johnny Cash, June Carter, the Tennessee Three, and myself to the Far East. I was a little nervous about this particular tour, because one of our stops was Vietnam.

Flying into "Nam" was like flying into any other airport. From the air the country seemed as beautiful and peaceful as Tennessee. We were met at the airport by the military who escorted us to Long Bihn Air Base in Saigon. Driving through the town, we could see the marks of war on the innocent. Young children with swollen stomachs gazed at our procession with eager eyes.

We didn't have to work our first night there and were assigned in twos to house trailers guarded by a soldier carrying a machine gun. Around five in the afternoon we heard our first sounds of war as big guns boomed in the distance.

That night I lay in my trailer. "Oh, God, why does this war have to be fought? Please, Lord, help us to get out of it soon. So many innocent people are losing their lives." The guns blasted throughout the night; it was hard to sleep so I spent most of it talking to God.

The corporal had told us to be cautious of any individual who did not wear a nameplate displaying his picture. That morning I was still in bed when someone moved quickly by my door. The guard had left his post outside the trailer to get a bite to eat, and my heart took off for the moon. What should I do? I searched around the room for something and grabbed my cowboy boot. I eased out into the hallway and snuck up on the person standing outside Bob Wootton's room. Drawing my boot back, I was a bit embarrassed to learn my dangerous intruder was a cleaning woman. The corporal could hardly explain who she was because he was laughing so hard, and I didn't mind all the kidding that followed.

John, June, and I went to the hospital to sing and play for the wounded. My heart was touched when the young soldiers tried to smile their appreciation. Some of them looked much too young to be there. But how blessed I was by the experience. That night I lay in bed thinking God had a job for me. I prayed awhile and knew what it was. The next morning I went to Colonel Castle and asked him if I could borrow a tape recorder to tape some conversations with the boys.

"Sure, Carl, I'll get you one. But why do you want to?" he asked.

"I want to call each family when I return to the States and play the tapes of their boy's voice for them. That way they can hear for themselves that their boy is okay."

"Carl, what a great idea. I'll get that recorder right now."

We left Saigon overflowing with memories none of us can easily forget.

As the airplane taxied down the runway at Jackson, Tennessee, I saw a huge crowd. It was unusual that so many people were waiting, unless some important dignitary was on the plane. Then I spotted Val, my children, mama, and daddy. They were all wearing big smiles. A red carpet was rolled out, and as I walked down the ramp, I was confronted by hundreds of my friends. I still didn't realize what was going on! The mayor met me at the end of the carpet and presented me with a key to our city and said, "Welcome home, Carl Perkins. This is your week, and we are all proud of you!"

Maybe it is not very manly to cry, but I could not help it. I cried like a baby. Val and I rode in the lead car of the procession that passed slowly through Jackson, and I stared at the long line of cars trailing behind.

That week was filled with unforgettable events, all thought up by a dear friend, Tommy McKnight. On Friday a special banquet was held under a banner that said "Blue Suedes Turn Gold." Different folks who had played an important part in my life presented a "This Is Your Life" program.

From behind the curtain a weak voice said, "Little Carl said when he was in the fourth grade he was going to be a radio star." And Miss Lee McCutcheon appeared, holding the cap and cape I had worn in the fourth grade band. How happy I was, and how grateful I will always be to the sweet people in my hometown for showing me such love.

After the excitement of the homecoming had ebbed, Val and I began calling the families of the boys I had met in Vietnam. I didn't realize how much hearing the voices of their boys would mean to them until I heard their weeping.

"That's really Danny's voice," one mother cried. "We didn't know if he was even still alive. I thank God that you called."

Val and I listened to each prayer muttered, and we

prayed and cried, too. It was in helping that we ourselves were helped.

About six months later the Cash Show was in Montgomery, Alabama. The stage guard came to my dressing room and said, "Mr. Perkins, there are some people at the stage entrance to see you. They won't go away until they talk to you."

I went to the stage door, and there stood a boy I had talked to in Vietnam. He was from Montgomery, and was with his girl friend and folks. They wanted to thank me in person, but it was I who thanked them for the blessing I had received. I got seats for them beside the stage, and as I performed I looked over at their happy reunion. My voice almost broke.

As my concerns for others grew stronger each day, opportunities to serve my fellow-man opened up. I became active in my church and was elected president of the Methodist Men.

That Christmas the family and I decided we would not spend a lot on gifts for ourselves. Instead, we decided to fill plastic bags with fruits, candies, and nuts and a note saying, "Merry Christmas. Somebody loves you," and pass them out to poor kids.

After church one Sunday before Christmas we began driving through the streets of Jackson searching for kids who appeared to be in need, when we found ourselves in the housing project we had lived in before the days of *Blue Suede Shoes.* I parked the car and opened the trunk, stocked full of goodies. Children seemed to fall from the sky. They were everywhere, and as quickly as they had come, they disappeared. The trunk was empty. I stood there for a moment and looked over to the apartment where Val and I had lived. I vividly recalled that Christmas morning when Stan's little red wagon turned over on him, and I cried a little. God had answered my prayer that morning by blessing abundantly so that I was not only able to give to my own children but to many others also.

Yet with all our happiness, there were still times of sadness ahead. It was Christmas again a couple of years later. I had left home to do a show in California with Johnny Cash. As I stepped from the plane at the airport in Los Angeles, a man approached me.

"Are you Carl Perkins?"

"Yes, I am." I replied, and he handed me a number to call.

I called, and Johnny answered the phone.

"Carl, are you sitting down?"

"No, John," I laughed, "I'm kinda tired of sitting. I've been sitting down since we left Memphis!"

"Son, I've got some bad news. Your brother Clayton has been shot!"

"What did you say, John?"

"Clayton's been shot!" he repeated.

"How bad is he?"

"He's killed himself."

The phone left my hand. Clayton could not be dead. I had just seen him earlier that day, and he was alive and well. W. S. returned home with me, and we met the despairing faces of my family at the door.

"Val, what happened?" I asked, not wanting to know.

"Well, Carl," she said, as tears welled in her eyes, "Greg went over because Aunt Nell called, and he found Clayton's body in the bedroom. The coroner said he had been dead about three hours. There was no note . . . nothing. We don't know why he did it." She cried.

"Who told mama and daddy?"

"Debbie drove up to the farm to bring them here. Your dad was not feeling well, and he didn't want to come, but she convinced them to anyway. God must have ridden in that car with her because she made it home without breaking in front of them."

Mama and daddy were greatly saddened, but they found the strength to face the tragedy! God had His hand on them.

After the funeral I searched Clayton's apartment thoroughly to ease my mind. As I took down the Christmas tree Clayton had put up just a week before, my thoughts returned to the last few weeks of his life. He had undergone surgery because of a stomach disorder. While he was in the hospital, I talked to him about his drinking. "Clayton, God helped me give it up, and He can help you, too."

I continued to witness to him about the saving grace of our Lord as I had done many times before, and Clayton seemed to listen this time. After he was released from the hospital, he began to change. He stopped drinking, and he had a glow about him. He came to visit me often. We would listen to the songs we had recorded back in the fifties and laugh at the difference in the sounds of then and now.

Like me, Clayton's total personality changed when he drank. After I stopped drinking, I did not want to see Clayton when he was. We drifted apart, but our brotherly love never did. The last few months of his life I enjoyed being around him.

Three days before his death, Clayton had said to me, "Carl, come out to the car. I have something I want to give you."

He gave me a small pine tree growing in a beautiful pot. I recognized it as the one Johnny Cash had sent him while he was in the hospital.

"Clayton, I can't take this. I know how much it means to you."

"Carl, that's just it. It means so much to me that I want you to have it."

I still have his gift of love.

Clayton had often told me he felt he had cancer, and I had tried to convince him that the doctors said he didn't.

Now I stared at the empty whiskey bottle laying on the nightstand beside his bed. "Oh, God, could it have been he didn't want to live thinking he would have to suffer the death of cancer? Could this have been the reason he drank again—the reason he took his life?" Only God knows the answer, but it is a wonderful consolation for me to have seen the change in my brother's life before he died.

Suicide is mysterious and very painful for those who are left behind. I pray you will never lose a loved one this way. But if you do, just remember God saw me through those times and will do the same for you.

In May, 1974, dad's back began to bother him constantly. The doctor said he had a ruptured disc. They operated and said within ten weeks he would be fine. The ten weeks passed, and dad was worse. I knew if anyone could help him, it was Dr. Barnett, the doctor who had saved my hand.

"Carl, there is definitely something wrong with your dad's back, and I intend to find out what it is," Dr. Barnett promised.

A couple of days later he called me and said, "Carl, your dad has cancer. There's very little we can do. The cancer is located in the bone marrow. Cobalt will kill some of the cells, but I'm afraid it won't stop the growth completely."

"Doc, how long?"

"It's difficult to say. I can't say how long he has had it. I would say, at the most, six months."

After I hung up the phone, all the pains of Jay's tormenting death flashed before me.

"God, please don't let daddy suffer the way Jay did. Please, Lord," I cried.

I decided then to spend every minute I could with dad. I called Johnny and told him I would not be traveling for awhile. He understood.

By September, dad's life was fading rapidly. I knew that soon I would have to give him back to the Lord. Each morning I drove up to the farm to see him. Worry began to gnaw at me. What if he were to need me during the night? Would I be able to travel the thirty miles in time? I talked to mama and daddy about moving from the farm to a small apartment up the street from us.

"Dad, we'll just lock up your little house, and when you get better I'll bring you back. That way I can spend more time with you."

"Son, I don't want to leave, but if it will make it easier on you, I'll go. But before we leave I want you to do something. Get you a shovel and go to the barn. Go to the front stall and dig in the righthand corner. There you'll find a fruit jar with some money in it. It's not much, but I've been saving it to put myself away with. I don't want to be a burden on you. You take that money and pay for my funeral."

I cried as I opened the fruit jar containing daddy's savings. Shortly afterwards the ambulance came to carry him to Jackson. Mama climbed into the ambulance with him, and I took his little dog with me in my car. As the ambulance pulled out onto the main road, dad raised his frail body and waved a sad good-by to his little house and farm. And at each house we passed I saw dad's neighbors standing in their yards waving good-by.

Dad was liked by everyone. He transmitted sparks of love through laughter. After his health began to fail, he suffered the agonies of a man who was unable to support his family. It was then he turned to that deceiving crutch, alcohol. As a child, I wondered why daddy drank. At that time I didn't realize what the emotional pain of being poor could do to a man. A few years before the cancer hit, daddy told mama, "If Carl can quit drinking, I can, too."

I always wondered if he really had. A few weeks before his death he told me, "Carl, after I'm gone there's something I've got that you might want. I ain't got nothing in the way of riches to leave you, but you might want this. Under a bale of hay in the barn is the last whiskey bottle I drank from. You are the reason I quit, son. I just thought you might like to know I did quit just as I said I did."

The day before his death I had to go to the farm to feed the stock. I was throwing some hay out to the cows when I had a thought—*Carl, throw that first bale in the corner out.* I obeyed, and under it lay the whiskey bottle dad had told me about.

Carl, your dad did quit drinking, and I led you here to see that last bottle.

My father was a poor, uneducated man who was not seeking riches in gold, but wealth only God can give. A few days before his death I was to perform at a benefit for cancer victims. I knew for some reason God wanted me to go see daddy before the show. I arrived at the apartment and found him suffering terribly as cancer silently destroyed the bones in his back.

"Carl," daddy said, "take these five one-dollar bills to the benefit. Maybe they will help someone to not have to suffer the way I have."

That night I closed my show with *What a Friend We Have in Jesus.* When I walked off the stage, I laid those five one-dollar bills on the stool, after telling the audience what my father had said. Let me tell you, the spirit of the Lord moved, and there was not a dry eye in that auditorium; those five bills were multiplied to take the pain from death's victory.

In January, 1975, I sat by daddy's side watching life slowly leave his body. There was nothing I could do but pray. Before daddy drifted away into a deep coma, he looked at me and said, "Son, don't worry. I'm ready to go. Me, Jay, and Clayton will have your guitar tuned and ready to go when you get there. We'll be together again."

Daddy's death did not leave me with that empty feeling I had experienced when Jay died. I knew he was no longer in pain, and I could just hear him saying, "Carl, this is the most beautiful place you could ever imagine." I knew He was with the Lord.

Yes, it is hard to give those you love back to God, but I want to see my brothers and dad again, so I am going to live each day for God's glory. And,

One of these days, and it won't be long,
I'll rejoin them in a song;
I'm gonna join the fam'ly circle at the throne.

THE BIRTH OF C.P. EXPRESS

On August 10, 1975, the Johnny Cash group was performing in Buffalo, New York. We were on stage, and I turned to Marshall.

"Marshall, you better give it all you've got, 'cause this is the last time you'll play bass behind me."

Marshall looked at me a bit puzzled. "Carl, what do you mean?"

"I just got

this feeling, Marshall. This is going to be my last time." I didn't know why, but I felt God wanted me at home.

Val had been having some trouble swallowing. The doctor said a goiter in her throat was causing the problem.

I arrived home from the tour and admitted Val to the hospital. The next morning Dr. Baker Hubbard removed the goiter in a two-hour operation. As I sat with Val's sister and our preacher in the waiting room, I knew something was wrong. The doctor appeared at the door and motioned me to come.

"Carl, don't get upset, but I ran into a small problem with Val's surgery. It seems there was a little knot in her neck along with the goiter. I cut it out, and it looks like it could be cancer. We'll know for sure in a couple days. I don't think there is any reason for undue alarm because I did get it before the membrane broke. But we'll have to wait and see."

I was scared. I could not lose my Val to cancer! I didn't tell anyone what the doctor had said. I just began praying and believing God would take care of her. When they brought Val back to her room, it was hard to fight back the tears when she asked if she would be all right. I sat by her bedside two days and nights praying that the news would be good. Dr. Hubbard came to the room after the analysis of the knot had been made and whispered, "Carl, it was cancerous, but I don't feel you have anything to worry about. We got it in time."

Val recovered from her surgery very quickly after we brought her home. I was so thankful God had heard my prayers.

Val and I had often talked about how wonderful it would be for me to have a band that included our sons. I asked my boys how they would feel about playing and eventually traveling across country doing shows.

"Dad, we'll try it. We may not be good enough, but

we'd love to try," Stan said.

Stan was the oldest, 22, and had been playing drums around Jackson for local bands. Greg, the youngest, 17, had been playing the electric bass and guitar since he was ten. Steve, 19, was just getting interested in drums.

I knew if God wanted us to form a band He would open the doors. We began looking for a piano player, and Lee McAlpin, an old friend and fine keyboard artist, accepted my invitation. Then God led us to David Sea. One night Val and I went to a Christmas party where Dave was playing. I was amazed at his talent and asked him to join us. He played saxophone, harmonica, guitar, and sang well. So we all got together, practicing many long hours in a studio I had recently bought. Stan's wife, Judy, who has a beautiful voice, consented to sing a couple of songs in the show.

At last we were ready!

On January 14, 1976, we accepted our first booking—a show with Willie Nelson in Alexandria, Louisiana. Before the show the group stood waiting behind stage, and I saw they were frightened. I knew there was only one thing that would change that!

"Children, let's talk to God," I said.

We bowed our heads and prayed God would walk out on the stage with us and that we would be the best we could be for His glory. God not only walked out on the stage with us, but He played and sang that night as well. "The C.P. Express" received a standing ovation, but it was God who deserved it. And we knew it.

The following night we were booked in Jackson. I didn't think any of us could be more nervous than the first night, but we were. I had not played a show in my hometown in nearly ten years, and as I walked onto the stage I faced an auditorium full of friends I knew and loved. I have been on many stages since my first performance in second grade, but never have I felt the love I felt that night in Jackson. Love was bouncing from each of us on stage to the audience and back. As the show drew to a close, the people gave us a warm standing ovation. I had chosen a song to do for an encore in case I needed one, but it didn't seem to fit the mood. I walked back to the microphone and said, "God, this is Your show and let this be Your song."

God told me to sing a song I had never sung before on stage.

"Friends," I said, "While you're on your feet, sing with me, *God Bless America.*"

Well, we took every booking we could get the rest of that year, but most of them were in the same southern honky-tonks I'd played in twenty years before. The crowds liked us, and once in awhile someone would come up and ask, "What in the world are you doing playing in a place like this?"

I'd smile and say I had a date to fill or something, but inside it would cut me. Sometimes I'd sit in our trailer while my sons were warming up the crowd and I'd talk to God, "Lord, my little ol' boys are in there playin' their hearts out for me. They're watching men pawing someone else's wife or falling down drunk—I wish they didn't have to see all that. Those drunks don't care what we do or how good we sound—why can't we perform where we can do more good, where we can talk about You from a concert stage? I want to call out Your name, and I don't dare to here."

Later, on the way home, I'd be driving and I'd look at my boys wiped out from fatigue and I'd start to feel bad. "Lord, I complained again tonight. Look how wonderful You are. Who in this world has been down as many crooked roads as I? I've done You so dirty and still You love me so much—You even got me wrapped up with my own kids, making music. Well, that's all right. We'll play at a honky-tonk tomorrow night, 'cause You got a reason for this. And, Lord, I'm sorry for being hard on the drunks. I guess I got a short memory."

And my boys held up well. "Daddy, we don't mind," they'd always say. "We're young." And to assure them I still was, too, we'd play a little touch football every chance we could, but I never let on how stiff and sore it always made me. Those boys love me so much, and whether or not I ever make it big again, I know nothing will matter as much as knowin' how much they love me.

When Ron Rendleman came down to talk about this book, he said some very timely things. I remember we were sitting in my den with a tape recorder, and I was telling how I felt God was holding me back. He looked at me and chuckled and said, "Carl, I believe you've got nothing but sunrise ahead of you. It's going to come. You'll see. Maybe God's got you playing in honky-tonks to show your boys how rough this business can be. You know, nothing spoils a young person quicker than to get too much too quick without having to struggle for it. Do you really believe they could handle fame right now?"

I thought a moment and had to confess that they probably weren't ready. Now, when I'm tempted to murmur, God brings Ron's words back to me—"Do you really believe they could handle fame right now?"

Well, Ron's experiences in being bold for the Lord rubbed off a little, and after he left I said to Val, "You know, hon, I'm gonna start singing about the Lord in those honky-tonks—we'll just see what happens."

Two weeks later we had a date to do in Mount Pleasant, Michigan. The place wasn't quite full for the afternoon show, and the Lord began to squeeze my heart. So at the end I said, "Friends, today is Sunday. Now, don't think I'm goin' to preach at you, 'cause I'm not. I don't want you to feel guilty. Feel happy—if that's the way you are, that's the way I want you to be, and that's the way my Boss Man wants you to be. I'm working for the Big Man in the sky now. And it's the greatest thing that's ever happened to me. He got us here today, and He's gonna' get me and my boys back home again. And He's the reason you're all here. So I just want to sing you a couple songs that mean a lot to me. Clap your hands with me, be happy. Don't feel bad. Feel good!"

I started with *Old Time Religion,* and after I got them clapping and singing, too, I said, "Well, listen to you sing. That sounds beautiful to me—can you just imagine what it must sound like to God? Here you are in a night club singing to Him—now don't you ever quit!"

Well, when I finished the medley, they stood up and clapped, they mobbed us, some wanted to hug us. But there was one fellow I remember in particular who followed me out to the parking lot. "Are you gonna' do the same show tonight?" he asked.

I swallowed, not knowing what he had in mind. "Well, yes, I thought we might." I waited and watched, and when he stuck out his hand I flinched a little inside. I could see something shiny in it.

"I hadn't planned on coming back tonight, but if you're gonna' do the same show, I'll be here. I want you to have this—I won't be needing it any more." He handed me the most wicked-looking pig sticker in the world, with a big old blade. Then, for the first time, I noticed the tears. I encouraged him to follow the Lord. Later, I put the knife on my mantel at home as a reminder of someone who was helped because I had obeyed God.

God spoke again about the evening show, but I began to have doubts. I said, "Lord, let me be. I already hit a lick for You. Tonight's crowd will be drunker and more rowdy, so I think I should keep my mouth shut."

But He wouldn't let me be. Come show time there were 350 in the room, standing along the walls, some even on the tables to see better. I did the same show, and they loved it—even called me back for an encore, so I did the medley all over again. And all the way home our old bus was touching the clouds.

"See, I told you," Val said when we returned, "God's surely got something up His sleeve for you. You'll see."

I know she's right. But I get so impatient sometimes I could spit. I was impatient to be an entertainer, to write songs that would touch folks hearts; and after I did that, I grew impatient again and frustrated and almost killed myself with alcohol.

When I began walking down God's highway, I wasn't content with walking along with Him; I kept trying to hitch a ride because He was always taking His time! But I know my day is coming. I've promised myself I will not sign a contract that stops me from speaking my heart on stage. When the Spirit leads, I want to be free to hit a lick for Him. It may not happen at every performance, but that's not up to me.

I'm looking forward to the first couple of months in '78 because Mervin Con has me booked for concerts in Europe, and I'll have a free rein. Con puts on the big British Country Festival every year at London's Wembley Stadium, and it's now a three-day event. Big country stars come from all over the world. Some Americans think only they sing country tunes, but almost every country in the world has its performers and fans. Japanese who can't even speak English sing "country." They duplicate old Hank Snow records. Country music has undergone many changes, from rock to violins and sound effects, and though the purist may frown, such innovations have given it wider appeal. As long as the message and melody speak to man's heart, country music will not die.

For a long time they called me "King of Rock and Roll" because of *Blue Suede Shoes*, but I didn't invent the term "Rock and Roll."

There was a disc jockey in New York—Alan Freed—who used to be very big. He had gone to see Elvis Presley perform and said over the air, "That boy rocks and rolls around the stage." And that's how the term was born.

Another reason I'm excited about Europe is what happened there year before last. The Dillards, Bobby Jo Spears, and her husband, Mike, and myself did a tour through England. Newspapers and trade magazine reports said things like, "The old Rock star—we wondered what he was doing on the Country Music Festival last year, but he sang country songs, mostly. This year Carl Perkins did his thing with his sons. He looked younger, he looked happier. The audience grabbed the old man and brought him back for three encores, which was the highlight of the six hour show."

From England, the boys and I went to Göteborg, Sweden, and again the reviews were good. At one performance the crowd was carrying on so that Dennis Weaver, the M.C., called me back and pleaded, "Perkins, don't you leave me out here all alone with these people."

Helsinki, Finland, was a carbon copy of the others. I looked around at my little old boys and saw their smiles after they'd put on one of the best performances of their short careers, and I knew something very profound and different was happening when we played.

I had an experience in Göteborg I'll never forget. I had just gotten into my hotel room from London. My phone rang, and a boy said in broken English, "Mr. Perkins, I have every record you ever made. I'm downstairs, and I love you because you love Christ." I knew this was something out of the ordinary. I hurried down to the lobby and met Vic. He was tall and trim and had long blond hair.

A lot of kids will tell you they have every record you've made, but he had them right with him. And clippings! He probably had every news item the *Jackson Sun* ever printed. Val has kept a scrapbook for me, and I thought hers was neat, but this boy's you wouldn't believe. Everything was laid out artistically and under plastic. He and his friend had come eighty miles to see me, and he told me he would not make the concert that night. I just knew he was going to say he didn't have money. I would have taken him to the concert with me, but that wasn't it.

"My daddy is dying in a hospital, and I had to make a decision to see him or you tonight," he said. "I know I must go to him, because this may be my last chance. I waited a very long time to see you; it was hard to know what to do."

There were a lot of Swedish kids standing around us in the lobby by this time—the word gets around fast. Most of them understood English.

"How did you make your decision?" I asked, guessing what he might say.

"Well, I prayed and the answer came to see my dad."

I looked around at the kids. They were hanging on every word. "You asked me a while ago why I believe in God," I began. "You answered your own question just now. I found out about ten years ago that after you commit your life to Christ, you can always count on Him to hear your petitions. The answer may not always be what you expect, but He does answer each one in His own time and way. After you prayed and got the answer, it wasn't so bad that you wouldn't get to the concert, was it?"

"No, sir, I had peace."

The kids got the point. I was so touched by this I went over and called my sons on the house phone.

"Boys, come down here and meet somebody. In fact, come down and meet about fifty kids who want to know more about God. That same God we worship in that Methodist church in Jackson is here tonight."

I love the audiences in Europe. My approach is simple: I don't know any other way. We'll do a whole lot of old favorites first, and then I begin to get serious. A new album that is being released soon has an example of what I like to do. My boys and I are playing, and I'm strumming on my guitar, and I say, "Now, my friends, I've come to the part in my show that is really what I'm all about. Through the years I have had people come up to me and say, 'Carl, where in the world did that rhythm come from that you use? It's different.' And I say, 'Well, it is different. It's different because it's country music with a beat, and I got that rhythm out of the cotton fields of Lake County, Tennessee. I got it by listening. I was trapped into listening because I had to work in those cotton fields. I listened to the black man sing spirituals. The old time spiritual. We had nothing to look forward to in those cotton fields. We knew we weren't going to make much money, but there was something about the hope and inspiration in those spiritual songs that rang out in that cotton field. They embedded themselves in me even as a youngun'. Here's a song my mama used to sing. I'm so proud today it never escaped me, 'cause it's got meaning for me even now.'"

Then I sing *Amazing Grace,* one verse, just me and my guitar. After that I step up the tempo and say, "Yes, this is the kind of music that I really love to sing. And here are some words I'd like to leave with you. I won't be saying much else, but I want you to take these into your heart and remember that I know you have problems here in your country and your town just as we do back home. We're always going to have them. But let me tell you, I know somebody who has the answers. Just listen to the words of this song. I want you to remember me not as the fellow who said 'Don't step on my blue suede shoes,' but as the man who sang to you about the only true friend you may ever have on this earth."

Then I go into my medley. My boys are playing in the background and I say, "My mama used to sing me these songs," and I sing *Down By the Riverside*.

"My mama used to say, 'Carl, just give me that old time religion.'

"See that? Feel that? 'Look, if it was good enough for Paul and Silas,' my mamma says, 'it's good enough for me.'

"There's nothing old about it. It's now, it's real, and ready to be accepted by you, my friend. It's older than time, but it's the best thing you'll ever get associated with."

At the end of that, while the boys are singing, I say: "And mama told me, she said, 'Carl it's good enough.' And, my friend, it's still good enough. For who? For me and you."

Then I bow and leave the stage. It's really the high point of the show. I might add another song sometimes, like, *Me and Jesus*

I know a man that once was a sinner
I know a man that once was a drunk
I know a man that once was a loser
But he went out one day and made an altar out of a
stump.
Me and Jesus got our own thing going
Me and Jesus got it all worked out

DISCIPLE IN BLUE SUEDE SHOES

Me and Jesus got our own thing going
We don't need anybody to tell us what it's all
about.

Sometimes the audience gets so quiet it's frightening; it's the same at the University of Chicago or Göteborg, Sweden. But the people listen to this old country boy who has an earthy way of speaking about God. And that's all I care about.

In April of '77 I was back in England again performing for enthusiastic crowds. One night I was up in my hotel room alone, looking at a park across the way full of trees. A lot of folks were out enjoying the warm spring night, walking hand in hand. I was feeling lonely, I guess, but words began to come, and I composed this song:

Take my hand and let me lead you,
Through this wilderness around you.
For there's troubles tuggin', I know, from all sides.
Please believe me for it's true,
The world won't ever get to you,
Take my hand and let me lead you
Through this wilderness of life.

There'll be many who will tempt you,
Tell you lies and then abuse you.
But don't listen to the roar of the lion.
For when the storms of life overtake you,
I'll be there and I'll protect you
Through this wilderness of life.

I'm your conscience and I'm talking to you now,
And I'm the last one in this world to let you down.
You can love me all you will,
Give me all you got to give.

My name is Jesus and I'll lead you
Through this wilderness of life.

I won't rush you with my words,
They'll be very softly heard,
But I'll turn you on the right roads you should take.
Though I'll never come on strong,
I'll let you know when you've done wrong,
Then I'll shine my light so you can find your way.

I'm your conscience and I'm talking to you now,
And I'm the last one in this world to let you down.
You can love me all you will,
Give me all you got to give,
For I am Jesus and I'll lead you
Through this wilderness of life.

ELVIS

On Tuesday, August 16, 1977, Elvis Presley died of a heart attack in his Memphis mansion. The world was shocked because his passing was so untimely—he was only forty-two. Thousands flocked to his mansion to mourn openly or to gawk and buy T-shirts offered by hucksters. Some countries even declared a national day of mourning.

DISCIPLE IN BLUE SUEDE SHOES

Val and I spent a sad Tuesday evening together because Elvis, though not a close friend of ours, did many things that indirectly aided my career. *Blue Suede Shoes* was aided in becoming a national hit because he had introduced it. He did more for country music than any man, with the possible exception of Hank Williams. They called him the "Hillbilly Cat" in the early days, and he rose from a $1.25-an-hour truck driver to a national legend before his twenty-fifth birthday. He really sang folk music for youth, just as Woody Guthrie sang for the dustbowl farmer. Elvis fused black rhythm and blues with the rebelliousness of white youth and made "rock 'n roll" a household word. The night he died I wrote:

Elvis, I sat down to write about you,
but it's tough to find a place to start.
Through my mind runs many things,
it lays heavy on my heart.
I remember the early years–
when our music was taking shape.
Our visits to disc jockeys just to get it played.
And I remember people saying,
"It's a fad, it's too wild, and it won't last too long,"
But they didn't know you, Elvis,
You were born to prove them wrong.

I could see it in the early fifties,
when our music was first played.
And I watched the magic of your magnetism
as I stood there beside the stage.
Our music was well represented
when you were on that stage,
And truly, history will record, my friend,
that you did pave the way.
You opened many doors for a lot of us to go through.

Thanks, my friend, you did it great–
my song called "Blue Suede Shoes."

They call you "king," Elvis, but we both know
there's only one.
And He called you home because His work for you
on earth is done.
He always had, and always will have dominion,
and you know that's the reason why
He called you home for that great concert in
the sky.

You'll always live among us, Elvis,
there'll be no death to your songs.
Thanks again, you were my friend and I'll miss
you–
now that you're gone.

P.S. Friend, there's one more thing I'd like to say.
A part of me and America died–when you passed away
today.

Yes, I am going to miss Elvis. For the last year or so I had a strong desire to see him. I felt a burden for him. I'd heard he'd become a recluse and wasn't taking care of himself. I wanted him to know he had a friend—a friend who had been to the bottom of life, who once had popularity and fame but who now is as content as he can possibly be. Sometimes now I lay in bed at night and think to myself, *Carl, why didn't you try to see him–God would have opened the door. You needed to let that old boy know you didn't need his money or his Cadillac gifts, but had just come to his house to eat corn bread and beans and a good strong onion and set and talk and say to him, "This ol' boy loves you."*

I don't think I'll miss many more opportunities to reach out to someone when I feel the Lord prompting me. I mean, those old friends need to know I love them, too, and that God can help them to a better life.

DISCIPLE IN BLUE SUEDE SHOES

I read a little book recently about a man who was concerned about all the starving people he saw in India. He said, "Lord, there are so many. There are thousands. What can I do." He grew defeated—the fire roaring within him became a candle flame. And God said to him, "Son, they die one at a time." So, he started to help them like that—one at a time—till God saw fit to provide a sponsor to expand his work. That's the way I intend to do it from now on.

But though Elvis was idolized, and fussed over, and treated after his death as though he actually were a king, he was only a man. A man with talent, a man with a big heart, a man with bushels of need for love and acceptance, but still only a man.

When someone who has touched your heart dies, it's always a sad time. But it hurts me to see how the world cries with the passing of a "superstar" like Elvis. For when its true King came to earth to suffer those thorns and nails for man's redemption, only a few showed up at His funeral. And today, only a minority of the world's populace really honor Him and live according to His teachings.

I've been doing a lot of watching and listening, and less talking, in the last few years and have learned an interesting thing or two about my fellow-man. Regardless of where he's from, he suffers from what I like to call the "super-star syndrome." Since he was created with a place inside him to be filled with the Spirit of God, but refuses to let God inhabit that place, he feels an awful emptiness and practices a form of idolatry—the worship of his fellow-man. It seems to be more prevalent in modern times—Rudolph Valentino, James Dean, Elvis, or false "Messiahs" like Sun Myung Moon are only a few examples. I have met folks all over the world—in English pubs, in southern honky-tonks, on college campuses—and basically, they're all the same. Deep down inside them is that vacuum. They wrap themselves up in new homes, cars, careers, science, education, or even loved ones. They remind me of an old granddaddy clock gone berserk, their pendulums swinging radically from person, to cause, to activity, trying desperately to find a purpose in life. I saw this first in the honky-tonks—people using alcohol, trying so hard to forget yesterday or tomorrow and just living for now: "Eat, drink, and be merry for tomorrow we die." The sad thing is—we don't die tomorrow. We live to eat the ashes of remorse and suffer the hangovers.

Every time we insist on going our own way, we switch off God's guiding light and begin to stumble around in darkness till we find someone who seems to know the way. We will, by nature, follow someone—if not God, then a "super-star" or a world "expert" who tells us how we should live, even what we should think.

I have learned the hard way that Jesus Christ is the only Superstar worth following. He is the only Expert who really has the answer to how we should live.

THROUGH A CHILD'S EYES

One night Val and I decided to take a long walk after supper. Shannon, our little three-year-old granddaughter, begged to go with us. We had been walking for a good while when we came to a streetlight that was out. It was very dark in the area around it.

I looked down at Shannon and asked, "Sugar, are you scared? Do you want your granddaddy to hold you?"

"No, granddaddy. I'm not scared," she answered. "Why should I be? I've got grandma on one side, you on the other, and Jesus in the sky."

I wasn't sure I had heard right. "Shannon, what do you mean, you've got Jesus in the sky?" I asked.

"Granddaddy, Jesus lives in the sky, and He loves little boys and girls that are good. He loves me 'cause I'm a good little girl. I love Him, too."

I will never forget how Shannon's words touched me. I was reminded of John A. Jones, a preacher of our church for a season, who taught me a lot about "childlike faith." The first time I heard him preach I knew God's hand was on him. I received a handful of blessings each time I was with him—his humbleness enriched me, his love guided me, his strong faith educated me. One Sunday he asked the congregation to join him in singing *Jesus Loves the Little Children,* and I can see the tears flowing now as he sang, "They are precious in his sight." He wasn't the only one crying.

When Clayton died, Brother Jones was there; when daddy died, he was there; when Val had surgery, he was there; and when I needed a friend badly, he was there. One time he told me, "Carl, when the problems get too big for you to handle, remember, they are just the right size for God." Brother Jones is now laboring for the Lord in Benton, Kentucky. If you want a blessing, go hear him preach.

Brother Jones has the kind of childlike faith I need more of, the kind of faith Jesus spoke of—"And Jesus called a little child unto him, and set him in the midst of them, and said, Verily I say unto you, Except ye be converted, and become as little children, ye shall not enter into the kingdom of heaven. Whosoever therefore shall humble himself as this little child, the same is greatest in the kingdom of heaven" (Matt. 18:2-4).

There was a time when I believed, like a lot of folks

do today, that we're all going to make it someday if we just try to do the best we can in life. I no longer accept that. The Bible does say, "God so loved the world," but there's no promise anywhere in it that guarantees salvation outside of Jesus Christ. "Except ye be converted, and become as little children, ye shall not enter into the kingdom of heaven," it says again and again. My life didn't make any sense at all till I started getting serious about God and became converted. *Converted* means to turn away from things that are wrong and seek a new life in Jesus Christ. And that's "the way" I got off Satan's one-way trip. I had to jump off his wagon in childlike faith, trusting that my heavenly Father would catch me before I ever hit the ground. And He did! Most men, it seems, won't do it because their pride won't let them.

There are mornings I wake up ready and eager to face the day for Christ, when an obstacle confronts me. For instance, since leaving Johnny Cash's show and having my own band, I have found making a comeback very frustrating.

Just when things seem to be going well, one of the bookers will call and say, "Carl, I'm sorry, the tour has been canceled." Or, the record producer calls to say, "Carl, I'm afraid this record is not going to make it." And the world seems to crumble around me.

"Why?" I ask the Lord, "when I'm trying so hard?" And He never fails to answer me through my family.

"Daddy, it's all happening for a reason. God is trying to lead you through that special door, and He's got to get everything right."

Or, "Carl, look how long God had to wait on you to become a Christian. Don't you think you can wait on Him a little longer?"

I know they're right. But it's hard to always have the faith of a little child.

DISCIPLE IN BLUE SUEDE SHOES

Some folks say, "God helps those who help themselves," and I used to believe that too. But as I look back on my life, I can see that, mostly, I was helping myself to everything I wanted in life. I've since changed my thinking to, "God better help those who think they can help themselves." It's too easy to get independent, even for a Christian who should know better. Stocks and bonds, insurance policies, investments for retirement, insisting that our kids get the best education to insure success in life can breed independence and dependence on the world rather than trusting in Jesus like a little child might trust his mama or daddy. Listen to Jesus' words:

> *"Therefore I tell you, do not be anxious about your life, what you shall eat or what you shall drink, nor about your body, what you shall put on. Is not life more than food, and the body more than clothing? Look at the birds of the air: they neither sow nor reap nor gather into barns, and yet your heavenly Father feeds them. Are you not of more value than they? And which of you by being anxious can add one cubit to his span of life? And why are you anxious about clothing? Consider the lilies of the field, how they grow; they neither toil nor spin; yet I tell you, even Solomon in all his glory was not arrayed like one of these. But if God so clothes the grass of the field, which today is alive and tomorrow is thrown into the oven, will he not much more clothe you, O men of little faith? Therefore do not be anxious, saying, 'What shall we eat?' or 'What shall we drink?' or 'What shall we wear?' For the Gentiles seek all these things; and your heavenly Father knows that you need them all. But seek first his kingdom and his righteousness, and all these things shall be yours as well.*

> *"Therefore do not be anxious about tomorrow, for tomorrow will be anxious for itself. Let the day's own trouble be sufficient for the day" (Matt. 6:25-34,* RSV*).*

Do I worry? Yes, at times. Sometimes I forget to take time to pray about problems, or even spend enough time with the Lord each day. If I keep my "hand in the hand of the Man" I find things are better, but if my hand leaves His, the devil somehow seems to get a new toehold in my life. Often, Satan reminds me of how easy it was when I drank my worries away. Immediately, when I'm tempted, I know I have to make a decision. I've learned that when I choose God's way, I receive power; saying "no" the next time is easier. It's almost as if God's not free to fight off evil until I use my free will. And when I'm victorious, I'm strengthened to fight even greater battles. The Bible confirms this: "There hath no temptation taken you but such as is common to man: but God is faithful, who will not suffer you to be tempted above that ye are able; but will with the temptation also make a way to escape, that ye may be able to bear it" (1 Cor. 10:13).

Life can often become a mixed-up state of affairs. Many times I wonder why things happen as they do, or why other things never happen. Discouragement would become my constant companion if I let it. And that leads to depression—like I used to feel when I'd think of the untimely deaths of my two brothers or the suffering and death of my daddy. But one day it occurred to me that being overly grieved over a loved one really smacks of selfishness—as if some personal property has been yanked away from us. Jay and Clayton were only my brothers, not my children. They were God's children and, therefore, His responsibility, not mine.

It's the same way with a lot of parents and their

kids. They keep forgetting they're only baby-sitters for God. Sometimes long after their child leaves home, they fuss and worry because their "property" is out in the world getting stepped on—when all the time it's God's property that's out there. They take on God's worries, and being incapable because they're only human, they end up with ulcers or worse.

Sometimes we get all flustered or rebellious because we don't understand. We demand to have God's knowledge rather than just trusting and being content with the understanding God wants us to have. When Jay died at twenty-nine, it was terrible for me. When I kept asking why and didn't get an answer, I grew rebellious and it about wrecked my life. If something similar happened today, I hope my reaction would be different because I've learned a little about trusting.

Many tribulations come our way to strengthen us, as a young oak tree is toughened by strong winds. God does not want incubator children! Suffering molds us into the image of Jesus if we do not rebel. A lot is preached these days about being joint heirs with Christ and sharing in His riches, but very little is said about co-experiencing His suffering. But the Bible says, "and if (we are) children, then heirs; heirs of God, and joint-heirs with Christ: if so be that we suffer with him, that we may be also glorified together" (Rom. 8:17). And why are we called to suffer? Because "as Christ hath suffered for us in the flesh, arm yourselves likewise with the same mind: for he that hath suffered in the flesh hath ceased from sin. That he no longer should live the rest of his time in the flesh to the lusts of men, but to the will of God" (1 Peter 4:1-2).

Whenever I get to feeling low, I'm often reminded of mama. She's been through a lot of hard living—lost a husband and two boys—and today she lives alone in a small apartment. But she testifies that the Lord's presence is always with her. My mother-in-law, Mrs. B. C. Crider, older than mom at eighty-six, lives alone also and can say the same.

I hope and pray that after reading this book you won't say, "It's nice that he got his life together," and put it up on the shelf and forget it. My main motivation in sharing my life story is so that folks will see the stupid things a man is capable of, and how great God's faithfulness and mercy are. Many of you are my friends. But most of you I'll never meet, at least not in this life, yet I love you and am concerned for you. I see Satan burning the midnight oil in people's lives, ripping them off through his angels of deceit, turning their heads to his lies when they should know better. Just like I should have known better had I spent more time with God in my early years.

But you know, friend, I'm so glad I've found Someone who never will rip me off. I used to get so down because it seemed there were so few folks I could really trust. But this Person I've found has never let me down yet, and He has a tremendous track record in mending broken lives, just like He did for me, setting people free from enslaving habits, and lavishing love on those hungering for it. He's come to town with a whole bushel of bread, enough for everyone. I'm just one beggar telling another one where to eat. If you'd like some of His bread, then all you need do is ask—He's got plenty for everyone. Now, you can grab a little and run, like a lot of folks do, or you can sit down and have yourself many a fine meal with Him—it's completely your choice.

I realize now more than ever that I am not perfect nor will I ever be. When comparing my life with those who I feel are really good Christians, I find I have only begun to live as He would have me to. But I am thankful

DISCIPLE IN BLUE SUEDE SHOES

I am aware today that the devil is out to get me. It's a fight to the end, and I'll fight with God's love till the end. Pray for me, as I will for you, because through prayer we gain power to move mountains.

Thank you for walking along with me a ways and for letting me share my life with you. What Christ did for me, He can do for you. Why don't you let Him come in?

I will sing His praises for ever and ever because I'm not the man I'm gonna be, I'm not the man I need to be, but thank God I'm not the man I used to be.

Your Friend

Carl Perkins